LETHAL HERO

By
ROLAND
PERRY

Oliver Books
USA/UK

THE MEL GIBSON

BIOGRAPHY

First published in 1993
Copyright © 1993 by Oliver Books
All rights reserved, Oliver Books
Printed in United Kingdom
by Butler & Tanner, Frome, Somerset
Oliver Books/Publishers

Library of Congress Cataloging in Publication Data
Perry, Roland, 1946-
  Lethal hero : (the Mel Gibson biography) / by Roland Perry.
  p. cm.
  Includes bibliographical references.
  ISBN 1-870049-79-9

  1. Gibson Mel. 2. Motion picture actors and actresses —
  Australia — Biography. 3. Motion picture actors and actresses —
  United States — Biography. I. Title.

Library of Congress Catalog Card No. 93-086030

This book is dedicated to . . .
Pippa Jane
Alas I Never Knew

Also by Roland Perry

Programme for a Puppet

Blood is a Stranger

Faces in the Rain

Hidden Power (The Programming of the President)

Elections Sur Ordinateur

The Exile (Burchett: Reporter of Conflict)

PHOTO CREDITS

TABLE OF CONTENTS

CHAPTER

1

THE BEGINNING

"There's a whole lot of people in one person"

Mel Gibson

Watch Mel Gibson with a child. In *The Bounty,* for instance, Roger Donaldson's disturbing 1984 adventure film, take a look at Gibson's face as Fletcher Christian, fondly bidding goodnight to the two merry little daughters of Captain Bligh, played by Anthony Hopkins. Or notice how, in Roger Spottiswood's misfired *Air America,* real warmth floods Mel Gibson's face when, as veteran pilot Gene Tyack, he hugs his two Amerasian children. It is simple and from the heart. He loves kids.

It must have something to do with the fact that Mel Gibson had a simple and loving childhood himself. As the sixth of eleven children he was surrounded by noise and laughter, inspired by a competitive sibling cameraderie. The Gibson children were amongst the lucky ones — kids who know, without questioning — that they are at the centre of their parents' world. Not because of expensive gifts or an elaborate show of quality time but because of old-fashioned discipline, care, respect for education and the unqualified acceptance that there's nothing in life as important as family.

Mel Columcille Gibson was born on January 3rd 1956, at 4.45 p.m. in the small city of Peekskill, on the Hudson River, New York State. His distinctive middle name derives from the Gaelic for "Dove of the Church". Mel's family lived in a modest clapboard house in the riverside hamlet of Verplanck, a mostly Irish-Italian community one mile south of the city centre. The area is steeped in history, having been originally settled by the Dutch early in the 1700s. Because of its location on a point jutting into the Hudson, Verplanck was strategically vital to George Washington and his troops during the War of Independence. Several important battles were fought in the vicinity and Washington spent much of his time there during the campaign of 1776.

Verplanck today is a community of approximately 2,000 people, still about the size it was when Anne Gibson was brought home from the hospital with her sixth baby in 1956. "It's the kind of town where people leave their doors open; everybody's in and out of each other's houses," says a resident. Like most of their friends and neighbours, the Gibson family attended St Patrick's Catholic Church, just up the road. A friend of the family remembers the Gibsons walking to church together up the hill, all the children quiet and well-behaved. Their house on Highland Street was across from the site of Verplanck's popular Our Lady of Mount Carmel Festival, an event that attracts thousands of people every year.

Over the years Verplanck has become known as "its own, separate place," according to one local. "Everybody there is either Irish or Italian, and they're all Catholic." Politically as well, Verplanck has always been its own separate place, as demonstrated by its record during the presidential election of 1928, when the returns from this Democratic-Catholic stronghold were overwhelmingly in favour of Alfred E. Smith against Herbert Hoover, a demonstration of complete reversal of the pattern of the national vote.

The citizens of Verplanck have never been afraid to defend their values, either. A Westchester County Historical Society chronicle of the period reads, "That same election evening, Ku Klux Klan leaders from Peekskill attempted to lead a motor caravan through the little hamlet. When the twenty cars of Klansmen came down the main street, the townspeople drove them away with bricks, bottles, sticks, stones and eggs. The Klan leader was beaten and sustained a bad cut on the head.''

The people of Verplanck today seem almost to echo this other era in their devotion to traditional American values, with a strong emphasis on the importance of religion, home and family. Despite its small size, Verplanck boasts a large volunteer fire department; the people there take care of each other. Values like these were shared by the Gibsons, and these simple, uncompromising principles, along with the readiness to defend them, have lived on in Mel Gibson in spite of geographical uprooting and exposure to the temptations of Hollywood stardom. When Mel was six, the family moved north to a large farmhouse in the rural area of Salisbury Mills, not far from the small town of Washingtonville. The house, which no longer exists, was part of a wooded bungalow resort overlooking Beaver Dam Lake. Because the region was farther west of the river it had been more recently settled than their former home, and thus more recently occupied by Indians. One land grant from as late as 1907 describes a parcel of land ''beginning at a point eighty-five chains from the wigwam of the Indian Maringamus, which was on the southwest bank of Murderer's Creek, just across the railroad track from the Catholic Church of St Mary.''

Mel Gibson was confirmed at this same church and attended the Washingtonville School, a six-mile bus ride from home. Washingtonville itself is a rustic little town that seems removed by both time and distance from the chaos of New York City, although it is only sixty miles to the north.

Life was full. "We didn't have a lot of money . . . but I had a happy childhood, surrounded by lots of trees and lots to do," Gibson remembers. "I was into dreaming. Dairy Queen. Rock throwing. Falling leaves. Climbing trees. I used to hang out with my brothers all the time, because there were four of us who were really close in age. There were rock fights, injuries, fistfights. There was spending the days in the top of an apple tree, just eating the fruit and dreaming." It's ironic to reflect that even as he speaks there are probably countless ten-year-old boys dreaming, in other small towns, among other apple tree branches, about growing up to be a hero just like Mel Gibson.

His mother, Anne, was from Brooklyn and his father, John Hutton Mylott Gibson, from the Midwest. Called "Red" because of his flaming ginger hair, he worked as a brakeman for the freight trains on the New York Central Railroad. One family friend affectionately describes Red as "the kind of guy you'd look at and you'd know he was Irish. He had the map of Ireland all over his face." A devout Catholic, Red Gibson is also a versatile and energetic man who was at one time or another a singer, a plumber, a successful quiz show contestant (one of the few grand champions ever on TV's "Jeopardy!") and a computer programmer. A religious conservative who as a young man considered joining the priesthood, he is fiercely opposed to the recent changes in church dogma (as is his son) and now writes books about ecclesiastical history, making an earnest, if unpopular, case against the reforms of Vatican II.

"My dad's a pretty cool character," says Gibson. "He was never an edgy, jumpy, nervous type of guy.

He's very capable. When I was a little kid, he taught me the Ten Commandments. After he was through, he said, "Now I'm going to tell you the eleventh commandment: Thou shalt not kid thyself."

And he hasn't. Mel Gibson has grown up possessing that same calm certainty, the grasp of reality. It can't have been easy for someone who was hit, at a young age, with fame like a swift right hook to the chin.

Red Gibson's television winnings had been enough to provide a more comfortable home for his family. When they moved to Salisbury Mills, however, the Gibsons found themselves among people who were neither Irish nor Italian, and not Catholic, either. Mel recalls, "We felt like we were on the outside." A school friend of Mel's older sister, Mary, remembers her as shy, quiet and a bit lonely. But James Hyland, who was a young English teacher at the time, recalls things differently.

"In the school system, anyway, the children were all very well adjusted, very popular." He goes on, "And they were conscientious, good students. Education was stressed in the house; it was a priority. The kids were expected to study and do their homework and take things seriously. They were a wholesome family; they had values."

Hyland remembers sharing an interest in Irish folk music with Mel's brother, Kevin, and eventually with the rest of the Gibsons. When the family left Salisbury Mills, they transferred most of their records to tape and gave their son's teacher their extensive vinyl collection.

They departed in 1968. Red had suffered a serious spine injury which had ended his railroad career. With the escalation of the Vietnam war and with no real reason to stay in the United States, he moved Anne and their eleven children to Australia.

It was a huge change for the Gibson children. Mel looks back on it now with respect for his father's spirit of adventure. "I guess it took a lot of balls, especially after he'd lived in America for so long," he says. "But his mother came from Australia and he wanted to get back to his roots."

Red's mother was Eva Mylott, a celebrated opera singer during the early 1900s. Mel Gibson's Irish good looks are apparently inherited from her. She was so talented a contralto that she became a protegé of the great Nellie Melba and was invited to study in Paris with Madame Marchesi (Melba's own teacher). A Boston review from 1907 calls her "a small, titian-haired singer" and *The New York Times,* in 1916, says her voice had "natural quality". A photograph of the elegant Eva Mylott in her prime reveals a noticeable resemblance to her grandson, especially around the eyes.

Eva Mylott moved to America and, in 1914, married Chicago industrialist Hutton Gibson, Mel's grandfather, but she remained loyal to her homeland. She rallied to its cause during World War I, donating medical instruments to Australian hospitals. Eva Mylott Gibson died suddenly in 1920 a few weeks after the birth of her second child, Mel's uncle Alexander.

It's romantic to imagine that the gifts of Eva Mylott live on in her gifted granson, or to trace Mel's charm to his Irish ancestry. His great grandfather, Eva's father, emigrated to Australia from County Mayo in 1862. True, in Mel Gibson's case, classic Irish charm has been tempered by Australian twentieth-century machismo and American cynicism, but the charm wins out on film, in characters like *Lethal Weapon's* tortured but cool Martin Riggs or the emotionally aroused Guy Hamilton in *The Year of Living Dangerously.*

His real charm lies in his lack of conceit — rare in any actor. You get the feeling that he really doesn't believe he's particularly good-looking, or special in any way. He's just doing his job. Being part of a large, energetic family must have contributed to this attitude. "When you're the sixth of eleven children," as he smilingly puts it, "you're either a realist or you're dead."

CHAPTER

2

THE SHAPE OF THINGS
TO COME

"I think it's good to be a hybrid. It's turned me into an observer."

Mel Gibson

Few people realised in 1968 that Sydney, Australia was about to become the vibrant centre of a creative new era in film and music. Its emergence into the mainstream of world cinema coincided with its political awakening — during the late sixties there were widespread, passionate demonstrations in Sydney and Melbourne protesting against Australia's involvement in the Vietnam War. A new artistic awareness seemed to parallel this political one, and suddenly, Sydney was an exciting place to be.

Encouraged by government subsidy and driven by boundless imagination, new Australian filmmakers began to surface on the world scene. For the first time, Australian films were achieving success at the Cannes Film Festival. By the early seventies, with irreverent and innovative comedies like *Stork,* directed by Tim Burstall (who later directed Mel Gibson in his fourth feature, *Attack Force Z*), followed by creatively arresting films like Peter Weir's surreal *The Cars That Ate Paris,* the Australian cinema was up an running. Later in the decade, powerful and beautifully photographed movies such as Gillian Armstrong's *My Brilliant Career* and Bruce Beresford's *Breaker Morant* firmly established Australia as an international player in the movie game.

When the Gibson family moved there, things in the Australian film capital were just beginning to percolate, but at this point, movies were the farthest thing from Mel Gibson's consciousness.

He attended a Catholic boys' school, St. Leo's Christian Brothers School, in Wahroonga, a north Sydney suburb. At first, the transition was difficult. Just absorbing his new surroundings at the impressionable age of twelve must have been a challenge. Street names like Warrawee,

Warrimoo and Warringah. Neighbourhoods called
Turramurra, West Pymble and Bobbin Head! (You
can almost hear the childish snort of incredulity and
see the blue eyes widen as they absorb the strangeness
around them). It was a far cry from Washingtonville.

And he was shy. "I had a fairly rough time of it,"
he says. "The kids made fun of me and called me
'Yank'." But before long he'd found his niche. They began
to called him "Mad Mel" instead, after a popular radio
personality. He acquired a reputation for doing off-the-
wall things, for being irreverent and crazy in public. On a
train, he'd pretend to be a monkey, trying to disrupt the
passengers who had their heads buried in morning
newspapers. He'd fall down the stairs just to see people's
reactions, or lie down in the middle of the street and play
dead. He was the sort of kid who elicited squeals from the
girls, admiration from the boys, and probably a prayer
from his mother. He enjoyed going as far as he could and
watching people respond. For an actor, it was an excellent
beginning.

After St Leo's, Mel and his brothers transferred to
another strict institution, the Asquith Boys' High School.
Of his teachers during those years at Catholic schools,
Gibson says, "They had a hard-line discipline; some were
regular sons-of-bitches, but some were wonderful men.
When I was there, I rebelled against it, but you've got to
toe the line sometime."

A friend from his days at St Leo's remembers the
school's reliance on corporal punishment and Mel
Gibson's reaction to it. "Three of us had a competition to
see who could be strapped most often in a day. Mel was

crazy. He won it easily. I think he was strapped about twenty-seven times.''

Mel Gibson acted formally for the first time at St Leo's, when he was about thirteen, in a melodrama in which he played the villain. His friend recalls, "He hammed it up really well, wearing the black cape and carrying away the damsel." Still, throughout high school Mel Gibson had no thought of pursuing an acting career.

He bagged groceries and worked at Kentucky Fried Chicken. He drank beer and played rugby. He surfed and generally enjoyed himself. And he found a willing audience in girls. He and his friends would sometimes play a game with unsuspecting females, another foreshadowing of his eventual career: "You'd go out, and for a whole night, you had to impose a condition on the encounter. You'd have to have a backup story. You were newly arrived in the country. I remember doing the 'shipbuilder from Glasgow' routine — 'Yew tell me where I kewd get a gewd cheap meal?' You made yourself inferior so they'd open right up to you. It was an interesting study in human behaviour. You couldn't let it drop no matter what happened. We used to pick up some girls that way. It worked like a charm. There was something in the mask." It could be dangerous. "But sometimes we were found out, and that was ugly . . . oh, really ugly."

One of his teachers at St. Leo's, Brother Patrick Lynch, remembers Mel Gibson as an ordinary boy. "He was not particularly remarkable," says Brother Patrick. In a way, you can almost imagine what he means. Mel was, and is, essentially *normal,* one of the guys. His striking physical personna doesn't quite match his personality. As

Gloria Steinem once put it, "His mystery comes from his ordinariness." Whatever you call it, it works on film. "What strikes me about him on the screen," Brother Patrick continues, "is that he is himself. He's not pretending to be someone else."

Perhaps this gift for natural behaviour comes from his own clear sense of himself. As John Lahr explains, "Part of Gibson's terrific charm is his clear-eyed acceptance of both his and other people's limitations." This sort of worldly wisdom in turn may have been a result of his cross-cultural growing up years.

"Having to shift cultures makes you an observer of everything," Mel Gibson says, "especially yourself. By relocating, you tend to look at the country and the people in it from a different point of view. It makes you an outsider. I don't think that's a bad thing. I like it. I don't think I'm easily fooled by things. It's not that I'm smarter than anyone else; I'm just not as easily convinced by the society's arguments. It's very easy to be brainwashed in America, which likes to see itself as the centre of the universe. Well, it's not. Being an outsider helps you to question. I just don't believe any politician or anything I read in the paper or see on any news programme. I'm sceptical."

Scepticism may be a firmly entrenched part of his psyche now, but he didn't start out that way. The transformation from shy twelve-year-old American kid to cool, easy-talking, easy-grinning, heartbreakingly handsome Australian heartthrob took only eight years, however. It seemed to come naturally. By the time he was twenty, life for the young lothario was brimming with possibilities, the scope of which he himself couldn't even begin to imagine.

CHAPTER

3

THE SEDUCTION

"I knew I was going to be successful. I didn't know at what."
Mel Gibson

The National Institute of Dramatic Art in Sydney is a prestigious acting school where the three-year curriculum is designed along the same lines as RADA in London or the Juilliard in New York. There's a focus on physical as well as intellectual training; a student must learn to fence, dance and otherwise control his whole body. He must develop strong vocal and breathing techniques through hours of speech and singing classes daily. He studies acting by exploring improvisational and formal methods. He learns about dramatic literature through both classroom study and in performance, with a strong concentration on the classics. In short, he or she becomes disciplined.

When Mel Gibson graduated from high school in 1974 — as he puts it, "I just managed to limp out" — he had absolutely no idea that he'd go into acting. He was toying, not particularly enthusiastically, with the idea of journalism. He also had a tentative urge to become a chef.

One of his older sisters had more foresight. She'd watched him coming of age and had a sense of his possibilities as an actor — he was a natural performer. Without his knowledge, she requested an application from the National Institute of Dramatic Art, filled it out, signed with his name and sent it back, along with the five-dollar registration fee.

When his sister finally confessed what she'd done it, Mel was not pleased. "I didn't really go for it much. But then I sat down and said, "Well, why not? Why not two days out of my life?' "

It meant going for an audition, which meant memorising audition pieces. Like most drama schools and companies, NIDA required one classical and one contemporary piece, each approximately three minutes in length. He chose a speech of Edmund's from *King Lear* and one from *Death of a Salesman*. A few years later, coincidentally, as his star was rising, Mel Gibson played a memorable Biff in a hugely popular production of *Death of a Salesman* at Sydney's highly respected Nimrod Theatre. This early indication of Gibson's knack for choosing the right role has been repeated throughout his career. Whatever can be said about his films, one truism is that he always seems to be perfect for the part.

The audition was to be before a committee of teachers and directors. As the time drew near, Mel did what most young aspiring actors do before a big audition. He fought panic.

"I went to the audition scared," he remembers. But inexperience, and his innate confidence, were on his side. As he entered the room, he thought, "Who gives a shit?" "I just went in and just didn't give a damn all over the place." As any successful actor knows, that attitude — that discarding of pressure, anxiety, desperation — is the real key to acting effectively. Whatever else you possess in the way of talent, what you need to have in order to express it is relaxation, even a kind of casual cold-bloodedness, so you can let go and let it out. Mel Gibson has always had this ability, and it's what makes his performances so enjoyable to watch. He gives a damn about a lot of things, like the rest of us, including ideals, family, his character's feelings. Unlike the rest of us, what he doesn't really give a damn about is how he himself is perceived. In show business that can be pure gold.

And the panel of auditioners at NIDA knew it. They thought they saw something in this raw young man, and they were interested. The head of the committee asked the question he had asked all the other hopefuls, a question equivalent to the dreaded essay on most college applications. It was a question they were accustomed to getting eloquent, well-rehearsed answers to.

"Why do you want to become an actor?"

After only a second's hesitation, Mel replied, "I've been goofing off all my life. I thought I might as well get paid for it."

He entered NIDA in the fall, one of only twenty new students accepted that year. It was hard work, and not what he was accustomed to. "I went from playing rugby one week to going to dance classes in black tights the next. I was exposed to a whole new world of ideas. I was a little open-mouthed about everything."

His teachers remember him with amused affection. "He was quite shy," recalls Aubrey Mellor, one of his tutors who is now Artistic Director of the Royal Queensland Theatre Company. "And he used to tell stories about his family. He obviously had an immense pride in his parents, particularly his Dad. You could tell he came from a warm and loving home."

The overall impression he made seems to have been one of appealing naïvety mixed with undeniable talent. "Yes, he was shy," remembers Richard Wherrett, one of his tutors. "He was also a star in the making."

Mellor found him positively self-effacing. "He never called attention to himself early on. Finally, we became a bit annoyed with his long hair," (it was the mid-seventies, after all) "and told him to tie it back. Then you saw that he had a mobile face; everything that was happening inside him could be seen on his face."

This facility to project what he was feeling, without

histrionics and without exaggerated theatrical technique, suggested to his teachers that he had a future in films. He had all the other requirements, as well. He moved gracefully, as a result of years of athletics, and had none of the physical quirks students often need to overcome with weeks of posture realignment classes. His voice was naturally deep, unforced and resonant. He could sing, in a pleasant baritone. Everything seemed to fit.

But Mel wasn't driven. It all felt a little wierd to him, dancing around in tights and hanging out with all kinds of people he wasn't used to. The circus-like collection of characters at a drama school — arty types, debutantes, stylish gay geniuses, suffering intellectuals — were people he found it difficult to relate to at first. He could handle it, but he wasn't sure he liked it all that much. It didn't feel like real life to him. It was confusing.

When the first year at NIDA was over, he got a summer job working in an orange juice factory. The hours were brutal; he left for work at 4:00 am and didn't get home until 8:30 at night. The job gave him plenty of time to think. Maybe a life in the theatre wouldn't be so bad, after all.

"I realized I didn't want to end up in that stinking factory. It really made me pick up in the second year."

He threw himself into the work, developing skills that later gave his film personality a unique twist. He loved doing slapstick, for instance. Aubrey Mellor taught Mel in a second-year comedy course. "He was way ahead of the others. Some would do more character work, but he would really do good physical comedy, Three Stooges and the Marx Brothers sort of stuff. He's one of only two actors I know in this country who are genuine slapstick artists —

he can do the whole pratfall thing, walking into walls, falling flat on his face. Most extraordinary.''

It became one of his trademarks , that ability to create physical "gags," even outside of class. Once he was hit by a car as he crossed the road in front of a bus, and saved a situation that could have been embarrassing, to say nothing of painful, by performing a spectacular stunt instead.

"The car wasn't going full tilt," he says. "I saw it coming. I went up and did this massive handstand on my briefcase on the hood of the car. The guy slammed on the brakes, and I went flying off the top with my briefcase still in my hand. I went through the air feet first for the longest time. It was kind of fun. I landed on the pavement on my feet and with the briefcase out in front of me. I spun around four times like a figure skater and then came to a clean stop. It was a really stylish stop. The people on the bus applauded.''

By the end of that year he had come a long way. But his inherent personality did not change. "He's still basically shy," says Mellor. "Mel felt secure in being someone else; he could be quite bold. And he has much more courage in his acting now.''

This can be said of many actors; their personality seems to be in complete contrast to the personalities they assume as a character. We've all heard about actors who stutter in real life, then on stage or ir front of a camera speak as smoothly as Olivier. Becoming a character is a freeing, non-threatening way to exercise all kinds of feelings and exorcise all kinds of demons. For the lucky working actor, it's the great escape, and what's more, it's sometimes in the name of art.

But art was certainly not the reason Mel Gibson stayed with it. He has never been a person with high-flown, intellectual, romantic ideas about ''art,'' Mel is the opposite and when he acts the two extremes meet in the middle and always seem to explode into sure-fire success. Positive and negative; real and normal against the contrast of imaginary and artistic, the combination makes both of them look good. It gives credence to romantic dialogue that this regular guy is saying it. As a moviegoer, you feel as if you're watching somebody recognisable, someone to identify with, and you buy the whole thing.

CHAPTER

4

THE CHASE

"Sorry, we haven't got a dressing room, you'll have to change in the open paddock there and buy your lunch."

Mel Gibson

NIDA gave Mel Gibson firm groundwork in the complex art of acting. By the end of his third and final year, his teachers and mentors had accomplished their aim, as stated in the school's curriculum, "to develop two complementary aspects of the actor's art: craft and imagination. Craft is that part of the actor's art which can be learned . . . but imagination must be continually enriched by improvisation and by observation and awareness, by contact with all the associated arts and by exploration of the creative impulse."

He'd appeared, as had his fellow students, in dozens of school productions. He'd had the opportunity to try parts that would never have come his way professionally, so he absorbed all kinds of stimulii and took all kinds of creative risks.

"I remember the first time I appeared on stage. I couldn't remember the lines and a curious thing happened to my knees; they wouldn't support me. And I had the shakes." But these symptoms gradually disappeared. "It halved itself each time I went on stage. The next time I was able to stand up and concentrate and remember, and the lines would come. Eventually it was just a matter of butterflies before opening night."

The object at NIDA was to provide as wide a spectrum of experience as possible for each student. "They did a production every three weeks and deliberately miscast you," he says. "I loved it." He actually played Titania, Queen of the Fairies, in Shakespeare's *A Midsummer Night's Dream,* almost too much of a stretch, one would think. (It's unfortunate for the world that at that time home video cameras had not yet become widely available.)

At this point, Mel Gibson thought of himself as a

"character actor." He was not interested in the parts played by romantic leading men, but in complex, meatier supporting roles. Mel had been successful in so many different sorts of parts and had had so much fun transforming himself into interesting characters, that he simply didn't see his own potential as a leading actor.

Aubrey Mellor remembers advising him, "You have a certain look, and when you leave here, people are going to grab you and use you for leading male roles. You are actually going to get those parts, and you should do them!"

To prove it, Mellor cast him as Romeo, opposite another talented NIDA student, Judy Davis, as Juliet, Mel didn't argue.

"He simply said he'd have a go at it. He might have thought Romeo was a bit of a milksoppy role, but he made it his own. He brought a wonderful boyish quality to it that was quite outstanding." Two years later, Mellor's judgment was seconded by director John Bell, who cast Mel as Romeo in the professional production of *Romeo and Juliet* at the Nimrod Theatre. Judy Davis also went on to make a brilliant career and is now one of Australia's most distinguished film actresses. She has been Oscar nominated.

During the first five years after graduating from NIDA, Mel did stage roles whenever he could, between what soon became increasingly frequent film jobs. He played small roles in *Oedipus, Henry IV, The Les Darcy Show* and *Cedoona* with the State Theatre Company of South Australia and was in productions of *No Names, No Pack Drill* and *Shorts* with the Sydney Theatre Company. He played Estragon in Becket's *Waiting for Godot* at the Jane

Street Theatre, and he returned to the Nimrod for their production of *Death of a Salesman* in 1982.

The *Waiting for Godot* experience was one of his favourites. It was done in circus/vaudevillian style, with lots of physical tricks and effects. "That part required probably the most physical strength I ever had to produce for a role. We did things that seemed to defy physics and gravity. It was discipline; it was fantastic."

Like many actors who have begun their careers on the stage, Mel Gibson appreciates the spontaneity and order of theatre work, as contrasted to the sometimes stifling technical drawbacks of working in film. "To get two hours of story on film, you have to work for two months. You can do it on stage in two hours; you're building something that all happens in the actual time you're there."

Theatre and Australian theatre specifically, is close to his heart. When the Nimrod Theatre was threatened with financial failure, Mel made a special trip from the States to join other loyal friends of the company who were organizing to help save it.

"Stage is a very important training ground," he says. "It solidifies the whole basis of acting for you."

The entertainment industry in the United States separates theatre on the East Coast from film and television on the West Coast, which in turn tends to create separate "species" of American actors: film actors, television actors and stage actors. Australia's entertainment community, on the other hand, was then concentrated almost entirely in Sydney. This made it possible for Australian actors, like actors in London, to alternate among all three kinds of work, probably resulting in better overall performances — and certainly less travelling expense.

So Mel Gibson did television. While he was still a student, he was cast in a soap opera called *The Sullivans,* and for Mel it was not a joyful episode. "It was a shocking experience — terrible scripts, no rehearsals, just knock it over in a day. I did two weeks' work, and I was on the screen every night for three weeks. I played a naval officer." Never at a loss for a pun, he quips, "I inspected navels."

Sydney's burgeoning film industry was also full of interesting and hair-raising learning opportunities. If you were an ambitious young independent film director in Sydney at that time, out to make a first stab at a full-length feature with the tiniest of budgets, the first place you'd look for talent would be NIDA. Such was the case with one Phil Avalon, an eager young actor, screenwriter and producer, who was also planning to co-star in the surfing movie he'd written called *Summer City.*

Avalon found most of his cast at NIDA, including a good friend of Mel Gibson's, Steve Bisley, who later appeared with him in *Mad Max,* another low budget film, but nowhere near as low budget as this one. Another friend, John Jarratt, was also cast in the film, and he in turn introduced Mel to Avalon.

Avalon considered Mel rather ordinarly looking and inarticulate. Since that was what the secondary role of Scollop called for, Mel was hired.

He received the princely sum of $20 for his work, and on location he slept on the floor, along with the other actors. He and Steve Bisley had to siphon gas from a wrecked car in order to get there.

To get back, they had to cash in a stack of empty Coca-Cola bottles. Luckily, they were all young, enthusiastic and full of mischief, so they made the experience more palatable by playing outrageous practical jokes on the locals.

Summer City (available in the States in a badly reproduced pirate version renamed, incredibly, *Coast of Terror*), opened in Sydney in December 1977 and was barely noticed by the critics. Set against the beaches of eastern Australia, its plot concerns a group of four friends, randy and looking for trouble, who go off on a weekend jaunt of surfing and general over indulgence. It's hard to tell if the film, which has the look of a home movie, is out to say anything at all, but it might be about friendship, hypocrisy and the double standard. It would make any feminist homicidal.

The conflict is contrived, the plot absurd, and the characters are completely unsavory. They all look as if they have a little too much makeup on.

Mel's eyes look weirdly dark in some scenes, as if his mascara is running, and his hair is a strange reddish colour, but the movie is supposed to be set in the early sixties, so that may have been a misguided attempt at achieving a period look. The acting is sincere, however, and Mel has a quiet presence that doesn't call attention to itself but manages to contribute just the same. He has one bit scene, on a beach, in which he extols the virtues of surfing: "It might sound stupid — it's a way of life, I suppose. If you've got any problems, or worries, or anything like that, you just take 'em all out there and thrash 'em out in the waves."

As awful a movie as it is — Mel calls it "a cheap, nasty flick, an abomination" — the acting is natural and believable. Although Mel seems a little self-conscious with his shirt off and slightly awkward a couple of times, he is generally able to transcend the material by not doing too much.

He does, however, have his first screen kiss, which happens to be in the backseat of an old Chevy with his friend Steve Bisley. It's just a playful, drunken, heterosexual joke, but it's the first of many screen kisses, and therefore worth documenting.

Fortunately for Mel Gibson better things were to come.

CHAPTER

5

THE BIRTH OF MAD MAX

"They say people don't believe in heroes anymore. Well damn them. You an' me Max — we're gonna give 'em back their heroes"

"Pete" Fifi Macaffee in *Mad Max*

Like all great commercial successes, *Mad Max*, the movie that put Mel Gibson on the entertainment map, was no fluke. It had Dr George Miller, now a producer/director of international renown, and the force of no-nonsense Australian producer Byron Kennedy (who was killed in a helicopter accident in 1979). The latter was not your usual avant garde film-maker, but a man interested in commercial success in the most unabashed way. Kennedy wanted to make films for the masses — the ordinary guys *out there* who were not normally consulted — or even kept in mind — when the new wave producers caused a renaissance of the Australian industry in the late 1960s and early 1970s.

Kennedy wanted to know what the mechanics in the local garage wanted to see up on the screen. He was in touch with the 'hoons' — Australian for local wild boys from the Western Suburbs, that is, the other side of the tracks. When hoons went to the movies they wanted to be turned on by the big, polished motor-bikes, violence and rock that was more of a noise than actual music.

The more urbane, cerebral Miller was the perfect complement to Kennedy, for Dr George was seeking the intellectual themes behind commercial success. He agreed that it was tied up with a Hell's Angels mentality, but in the early 1970s, that provided just the emotion. Dr George wanted the right story — the right line for the time. He asked an economics writer — James McCausland — to come up with a concept. His theme looked at the contemporary OPEC oil crisis which peaked in 1974, and the accepted myth of the time that the oil supplies might dry up. McCausland posed the question: what would happen if the oil ran out? What would happen if there was a world nuclear holocaust that isolated Australia as the only country — another popular myth — which would survive? Given these 'what if' scenarios. Miller and his writers went to work and took the concept to extremes. The basic script line in the end was nothing more than a way-out Western. Mad Max, the laconic outback outsider comes into town and takes on the violent forces of evil, the vicious gunslingers of a post-urban, post-nuclear era.

There were always going to be budget restraints and the setting for the film had to be in the rough Aussie outback, much cheaper than a city location.

So the main ingredients were conjured and mixed: a deeply violent goodies and baddies storyline for which the hoons would swoon; a substantial thematic background based on the oil crisis; and a cheap, but romantic outback setting.

For authenticity and research purposes, Miller, a practising doctor, deliberately took locum work so that he and Kennedy could attend 'trauma' road accidents. They wanted to know what a decapitation looked like. They wanted to see dismembered traffic-accident victims in their suffering state. According to Miller, some of the accidents were so bad that he had to enlist Kennedy as an assistant to save lives at the scene. *Mad Max,* reflected their experience, and undoubtedly one factor in its success was the astounding production values obtained from a miserable budget of $A375,000.

That money was raised by Kennedy from his hoon mates in his home territory in Melbourne's western suburbs. He went to his beloved mechanics and asked them for $5,000 or $10,000. The deal was straight-up and something the car-tuners understood. Money up front and a possible, eventual pay-out of exactly double their money and not a cent more (which every investor finally received, with plenty to spare for the producers). The hoons backed him and the tiny budget was put together.

However, it was a tough movie to get up. The script was shown to Phillip Adams, an early instigator of the Aussie film industry renaissance. He poured scorn on it, calling the themes 'right-wing, degenerate, decadent, and corrupt.' Kennedy-Miller, Adams said, had sold-out to nasty commercial instincts. He recommended that it should not be made. Because Adams — an advertising man — was the articulate film guru of the time, the funding bodies, which were nurturing most Aussie productions, spurned the novices. Their track record at the time had been restricted to several short films, including an award-winning satire on violence, *The Cinema Part 1*.

The producers hawked the script around, looking for co-producers and distributors. Not everyone reacted badly. One leading film company at the time, Hexagon, in Melbourne, wanted to go with it except for the fact that it didn't believe the stunts could be delivered as written without a much bigger — million dollar plus — budget. Kennedy-Miller was continually shunned as just another inexperienced movie-making team trying to do the impossible on the smell of an oily rag.

But they went ahead anyway. Finally Kennedy-Miller struck a deal with Warner Brothers International for foreign territories, and with one of Australia's major distribution chains, Village Roadshow, which agreed to underwrite the production costs.

When one actor in particular takes a cool look back at his mighty career, he should be eternally grateful to

Kennedy and Miller for their courage, drive and intelligence in following through on their dreams. He might also spare a thought for those Western suburbs hoons who took a big gamble, raided their piggy banks and put up the folding stuff.

They, in their own way, helped make it happen for Mad Mel as did three rather rougher hoons in a Sydney pub . . .

The big guy reached across the bar and elbowed Mel's ear as he gripped his drink.

'Hey, mate,' Mel said, 'be careful.'

The big man, about 6ft 3in, and with cauliflower ears, reminiscent of a rugby player who had seen too many scrums, scrutinised him and laughed gruffly.

'What's it to you, mate?' he said, giving Mel a shove. Mel shoved back. Cauliflower-ears put down his drinks, but before he could take a swing at Mel, his fat red-headed friend had done that for him. He hit Mel a glancing blow on the forehead, causing him to spill his drink on the third of the playful trio, a hard-looking, thickset man with a completely bald scalp. Nude-nut elbowed Mel hard in the side, winding him slightly, and enough for Cauliflower to punch Mel straight on the nose. He retaliated with two good punches to Red-head who was about to deliver a blow.

'You short-arse bastard!' Nude-nut said, surprised at Mel's tenacity. He thumped Mel in the back. Nude-nut kneed him in the side and grabbed at his face, trying to eye-gouge him. Seconds later, Red-head, groggy from Mel's punches added his weight to the fracas and fell on top of him. A barman called for a halt and tried to break up the affray, but all he succeeded in doing was to edge the grappling four to the door. Mel landed his third effective punch, crash on the nose of Nude-nut, who spun away holding his hooter as blood spurted from it.

Mel stumbled through the door out onto the pavement. The three assailants now pinned him against the hotel wall and kicked and punched him. Mel delivered one more effective blow, this time to Red-head, and that was it. He went down under a flurry of punches and kicks. Even when he lay semi-conscious on the ground the boots went in. His head and back were the main targets, before the barman, Bob, came to the door and yelled:

'Someone has called the cops!'

The three bashers give their victim one more bruise each for good measure, then moved off along the road.

An ambulance was first on the scene. An officer, Ollie Garrick, now of Cremorne, Sydney, remembers the scene.

'When we arrived, this guy was badly smashed up,' he said, recalling the night of October 11, 1977. 'I remember it for two reasons. First, until that point I'd never seen anyone so badly marked from a pub fight. He face was completely covered in blood, and his nose was hammered. His eyes were already closed from bruising and his mouth was full of blood. Our first task was to make sure he didn't choke on it. I remember thinking, as did the other officer with me, that this bloke might not make it. He was totally out of it, and I thought that there could be real damage. But that was for the doctors to worry about. Our job was to get him to hospital.'

They did and Mel took another few hours to regain consciousness. The doctor on hand stitched Mel's right eye and said he had to stay in hospital for another day at least because of severe concussion.

Late the next night, Mel remembered he had a cattle call for a film job. He waited until the next morning before deciding whether to turn up.

"I looked in the mirror and was still an unpretty mess," he recalls. "One eye was completely closed and my nose was a swollen mess. I still felt, you know, flat and a little groggy, but I thought, 'what the hell,' I'll turn up. The casting agent had my photos. They would know I wasn't normally like the Elephant Man."

As it turned out, Miller and Kennedy were looking for a no-name who looked tough and rugged. The star would be smashed about a bit in the movie and Mel walked in looking as if he had made up for the part. The casting lady, Mitch Matthews, took some video tape of Mel, who fumbled out an explanation for his condition.

"I thought you might like a few before and after snaps," he joked.

"Yeah," Mitch mumbled, as she looked through the camera at Mel. "Yeah . . . hey, Oh, wow! What have we got here?"

That night the tape was shown to Miller, who was more than a little interested in the look. Mel was asked to return to the studio ten days later, when his face had healed somewhat. He still looked battered, but Miller and the casting agent were then convinced they had found Mad Max.

"He had something," Miller remembers, "Mel *was* Mad Max."

Without the bar-bruisers' efforts Mel believed that he would never have got his big break in film. Such is fate. The twenty-one year old, just out of acting school, was on his way.

Mel's fellow graduate, Steve Bisley, who now teaches at NIDA, was cast in the role of Goose, Max's cop friend who meets an untimely and painful end. No one in the cast was well known, aside from Roger Ward, who played the part of Fifi Macaffee, Max's police chief, Miller wanted *Mad Max* to have no connotation brought to it from previous films or from television. His vision was "urban society in terminal decay. The inner city highways have become white line nightmares, the arena for a strange, apocalyptic death game between nomad bikers and a handful of young cops in souped-up pursuit cars."

Shooting on Mad Max began in October 1977, just after Mel's graduation.

"I was terrified," he says. "I didn't know what was going on." In the film, he looks impossibly young and angelic, which works effectively against black leather, violence and blood. Our first glimpses of him are teasers — the lower half of his face in a mirror, the reflection off his cop's sunglasses. As he gets out of the MFP (Main Force Patrol) pursuit car to check on the grisly death of the evil "Nightrider," we see all of him for the first time. The image sticks in the mind's eye because he's at once so intense and unnarcissistic, so collected and yet so on the edge. He refined this unique combination of characteristics ten years later for *Lethal Weapon,* and struck gold again.

It's a powerful combination. It's why Zeffirelli eventually thought of him for *Hamlet,* aside from the fact that his involvement in any film almost guarantees instant success. When Mel Gibson is on the edge, it makes his physical beauty more poignant; it deepens his impact. It's not the threat of danger from outside that makes you sit up and care; it's the self-imposed risks when you're worrying about Gibson's private demons betraying him, you watch him with baited breath until the danger is over.

The story of *Mad Max* is simple. Sometime "a few years from now" in the barren central wasteland of Australia, the social order is crumbling. What's left of civilization is barely being held together by an overworked and inefficient police force who are outnumbered by marauding motorcycle gangs and insanely evil car freaks who terrorize the highways. Max is a star pursuit cop about to quit the "rat-circus" and make a proper home for his beloved wife and child. His best friend, Goose, has been killed in the line of duty, and he's "scared of becoming a terminal crazy."

Steve Bisley, as Jim Goose, makes the perfect Mercutio to Mel's Romeo. Brash and smilingly careless, he is a cinch for a tragic death. His style in *Mad Max* is the exact foil needed for his friend's. He's part of the maelstrom swirling around Max's quiet centre, emphasizing Max's deeper tragedy.

Max says he wants to "get out while he's still one of the good guys." His chief, Fifi Macaffee, sends him on vacation instead, where his child is brutally killed and his wife mutilated by the vicious barbarian Toecutter and his gang of motorcycle maniacs. Max goes mad and diligently avenges their massacre by doing in every bad guy he can find. One by one, he hunts them down, engineering car crashes and roadside executions with cold-blooded efficiency. He doesn't stop until he's killed them all. It's violent exploitation with a comic book twist. Its themes have something in common with Charles Bronson's *Death*

Wish New York vigilante movies, so popular in the mid-70s.

The film's look is all sinister fantasy, its landscape laced with S&M and rusting metal. In this bleak void, the villains are one-dimensional and purely evil, the protagonist unbelievably superior. As one critic said, "Junky, freaky, sadistic, masochistic, *Mad Max* has a perverse intelligence revving inside its pop exterior."

It has a dark humour, as well, like the cinematic pun when Goose is "cooked," trapped behind the wheel of an overturned truck that is incinerated by Johnny the Boy, a Toecutter sidekick. In the climax of the film, Gibson gives Johnny an especially sadistic choice of how to die. He handcuffs the boy's ankle to the frame of a wrecked truck, arranging an overturned headlight so it begins to fill with a stream of spilling fuel. Max lights a flame and puts it within inches of the gas, and hands Johnny a hacksaw. "The chain in those handcuffs is high-tensile steel," he tells him. "It'd take you ten minutes to hack through it with this. Now, if you're lucky, you can hack through your ankle in five minutes." He drives away toward the empty horizon, finally having taken thorough revenge for his friend's murder.

Unfortunately, *Mad Max* was dubbed with bland, vaguely southern American voices for distribution in the States, spoiling the wild Australian feeling of the original. But Gibson's stature is clear; he's quietly powerful, cool, brutal and riveting.

The perfect tragic hero, he says his lines straight out, with no actorish embellishments. This style, like Clint Eastwood's, may not result as much from conscious decision as from simply not knowing what else to do, but it happens to be perfect for action movies. Like his character, Gibson gets the job done with no extra fuss. Just straight, clear and honest.

He presents the image of a domestic, loving husband whose halting inability to articulate his deeper emotions, is appealing and sweet. When tragedy transforms him into an obsessed, murderous avenger, he manages to do so with subtlety and a simple truth, not pushing the obvious but allowing himself, and us, to believe that it's a natural response to his pain. He says he was scared, but it doesn't for a second come across that way. Possibly Miller had exactly the right touch; in any case, whatever guidance he was given, it was effective, and whatever he was able to call up from his own resources, it worked because he sails through the requirements of Max's character as if they were second nature.

Portrayed by another actor, Max might easily have come across as either unrelentingly vicious or boringly self-involved. But as George Miller says, "Mel has an Australian quality. And it's difficult to be Australian and to be self-important. Mel will never be."

The film was shot in Melbourne, and from the beginning it was plagued by unforeseen problems. Before shooting even began, stunt coordinator Grant Page had broken his leg and his nose, in a motorcycle accident. Riding with him on their way to the location had been the actress hired to play Max's wife, Jessie. Both *her* legs were broken, and she had to be immediately replaced.

From then on, the shoot was a veritable festival of minor accidents and injuries, as intrepid stuntmen managed greater and greater feats of derring-do. Although

Mel did some of his own driving in the film, he wisely left the really dangerous stuff to stunt experts. And there was, indeed, some very dangerous stuff. By the end of filming, Miller, Page and their band of kamikazes had accomplished the incredible array of stunts that several advisers had predicted could never be done on their small budget, nor even by anyone outside of Hollywood.

Mad Max was an instant hit, at least in Australia, where it opened in 1979. For years it held the record of biggest-grossing film in Australia's history, and its cult status ensures its consistent popularity. It was greeted by the critics with intense interest, if not complete approbation. In fact, one often-repeated line from a review by Phillip Adams, who is now head of the Australian Film Commission, goes: "It has all the moral uplift of *Mein Kampf.*"

Other critics were, understandably, incredulous at the movie's impressive effects, its terrifying crashes and explosions. Jack Kroll in *Newsweek* wrote, "*Mad Max* is a straight fix of violence . . . it's a crazy collide-o-scope, a gear-stripping vision of human destiny careering towards a cosmic junkyard."

Miller was called "brilliant" and his film "a clever, effective, futuristic horror fantasy; one of the finest achievements of the Australian film industry."

Making the film had cost only $375,000 and it ultimately grossed over $100 million worldwide, as well as being the catalyst for enormous profits from its two sequels. And it was the vehicle made it heaven for Mel Gibson.

CHAPTER

6

ON THE EDGE

"He's aware of his limits. But you see, I'm not sure of what his limits are"
Piper Laurie in *Tim*

He stands back meekly in a crowd of rugged labourers, waiting for orders. Subservient, eager to please. The job supervisor tells the prim but attractive middle-aged lady that they're finished; he's leaving Tim behind to tidy up, and if she wants anything, just to see him. Tim gives her a shy nod. She levels a cool glance at him and looks away.

Piper Laurie plays Mary Horton, the lonely forty-ish woman who befriends Tim Melville, played by 22-year-old Mel Gibson. At first meeting, she doesn't quite trust him. He seems to her like some hot-to-trot young working boy who just might make a pass, or steal something from under her nose. Soon, she realizes that she's wrong, that Tim is, as he straightforwardly puts it, "not the full quid. Anyone'll tell you that."

Tim is slightly retarded, or simple as his family calls it. He's handsome, physically capable, impeccably polite and well loved by his parents and sister. But in many ways he's like a child. He's never learned to read, and left school at the age of fifteen to earn money as a working man. He's completely innocent about sex and the realities of life and death. He enters Mary Horton's world unexpectedly. The story was based on an early novel by Colleen MacCullough, best-selling author of *The Thornbirds*.

Tim's writer/director/producer Michael Pate was a well-known figure in Australian show business, having achieved significant success as an actor in over thirty Hollywood films. As a director, he was soon to win awards for a film called *The Mango Tree*, with Geraldine Fitzgerald. *Tim* was one of his first forays into directing, and a project close to his heart.

Pate saw *Tim* as a sort of modern fairytale. Pate had

become interested in its possibilities as a screenplay early on, although he had also been afraid the story was "too delicate, too improbable." He eventually decided it should be presented as a kind of allegory, "like the story of a princess in a white tower, and a frog that becomes transformed."

But then things changed. Piper Laurie was cast as Mary only four weeks before filming began, as a replacement for Julie Harris who had originally been signed for the part but who was now ill and unable to travel to Australia. Ms. Laurie's involvement altered the concept of the film. "It meant changing the whole script around. Instead of its being a more serious script, I made it a romance. And as Piper was fair-haired, I was looking for someone dark for Tim."

Mel was at this point working in Adelaide with the State Theatre of South Australia. Michael Pate had heard about Mel Gibson's work from his son, Chris, who was also a young actor. Pate got a look at the screen test for the part of Max that Mel had done for casting director Mitch Matthews, and was intrigued. Although *Tim* would be a big departure from a biker movie (a film that, incidentally, no one had yet seen), he thought Mel Gibson had a quiet power that just might work for the part. He flew to Adelaide to see if his son's enthusiasm for this *Mad Max* wunderkind was justified.

"I met him at the Festival Theatre in Adelaide and we had coffee. Then I took him up to lunch with some friends of mine who owned a pub in North Adelaide. They're a very down-to-earth group of people, and of course he got on very well with everybody."

Which brings to light another piece of the puzzle,

another reason Mel Gibson's career shot upwards as quickly and powerfully as it did. He "gets on well with everybody." To most people, who always see movies from an audience's point of view, that might not seem like a terribly important consideration. But the way the actors and other personnel involved get along together on the set can make or break a film. If a star is "difficult," as they say in Hollywood, it creates a kind of ripple effect of bad feeling that can hurt the process of filmmaking, causing both practical and creative problems.

On the other hand, if a star is easy to work with, reliable, hardworking and dedicated to getting the job done with as little fuss as possible, the film has a much better chance of being completed on schedule and within budget. In Hollywood, especially during a recession, *budget* is the magic word. That's another big reason everybody in the business loves Mel Gibson; for the accountants at Warner Brothers it's not as much his blue eyes as his blue-collar attitude.

Writer Jeffrey Boam, who wrote the screenplays for both *Lethal Weapons II* and *III,* agrees. "He definitely contributes to a good feeling on a set. No one is living in fear of being on Mel's 'bad side,' of suddenly being taken aside and hearing 'Mr. Gibson wants you to leave the set.' There's none of that kind of Hollywood prima donna bullshit."

So, having passed the "down-to-earth" test, Mel Gibson won the part of Tim and was given a release from the State Theatre Company. Filming began immediately.

The case was full of veterans. Piper Laurie had made her Hollywood debut with Ronald Reagan in *Louisa,* and had played opposite Tyrone Power, Rock Hudson, Van Johnson and Paul Newman. She'd been nominated for an Academy Award for her work in *The Hustler* with Newman and again for *Carrie* in 1976. Ms. Laurie subsequently received yet another Oscar nomination for her work in the film *Children of a Lesser God.* She was also highly respected for her television work, having appeared in many dramatic roles during the golden age of live television, including the original production of *Days of Wine and Roses.*

Piper Laurie was a little apprehensive about who was to be her leading man. She knew that the part demanded an exceptionally sensitive actor, as well as a very good looking one. Before she arrived in Australia to begin filming, she'd heard that Michael Pate had cast "this Mel Gibson, a local actor, and I thought, 'Oh, dear.' " She'd never heard of him and was now rather nervous about what his capabilities might be. After all, the entire film revolved around their relationship and the special qualities of the young man who was to play the title role. She remembers their first meeting:

> "I was standing in this [location] trailer in my *bathing suit,* that I'd been trying on for those scenes on the beach. And he was brought over to the trailer — we shook hands, and then I came down the steps. Well! I just took one look at that face, and it took my breath away. He became just more delightful as the time went on, and I could see how really gifted he was. But I knew, the moment I met him, that he'd be an enormous star."

Filming *Tim* was not a bed of roses. Michael Pate had six weeks in which to shoot the film, which is a very short time and demands excellent prepartion as well as a strict and efficient schedule. Piper Laurie feels that he was too ambitious, that he left a little too much to chance. "Michael thought he could do a lot more than he actually did do, within the given schedule. He rehearsed [to the extent that] it felt as if he thought we had a 20-week schedule instead; I mean that was the pace." Ms. Laurie remembers that it made their creative work "extremely difficult. And it was a difficult position for Mel, because he wanted to do the right thing, and he was sort of caught between his instincts and being under the supervision of someone who didn't seem in control."

Piper Laurie grew to admire the young actor for more than his talent. She saw that he could handle himself in a troublesome situation. Even at this early point in his career, Mel Gibson seemed to see the big picture. he wasn't as concerned about his own ego and his own problems as he was about the eventual long term effects of his behaviour. "I've seen actors in similar circumstances just go into a rage, get physically abusive," she says. "But Mel was very smart. For somebody who was twenty-two, besides being absolutely charming and of course beautiful, I thought he was very, very smart."

In *Tim,* Piper Laurie brings stature, dignity and a bittersweet vulnerability to the role of Mary. We see her dawning regard for Tim as a kind of awakening, an epiphany of generosity. She's never sentimental, always believable. It's a lovely performance, carefully crafted and truthfully executed.

Also in the cast is Australian actor Alwyn Kurts, who gives a touching and humorous portrayal of Tim's uneducated but loving father, fond of his pint and devoted to his family. Tim's mother is played by Pat Evison, a wonderfully craggy-faced, blowsy woman who brings a poignant reality to the part. Tim's sister, Dawnie, is played with sensitivity by the young Australian actress Deborah Kennedy.

This ensemble of fine actors made a nearly implausible story work on a deeper level than one would imagine might have been possible. They give a feeling throughout that they are a team of players who have a mutual understanding of the situation; they're not going to allow themselves to sink into predictable soap opera behaviour; they've got too much integrity for that. It is as if they've taken an unspoken pledge to rise above their material.

Mel Gibson's performance is restrained where it might have been blatant, rings true where it might have moments where it could have cloyed. His Tim Melville is free of all the irritating little mannerisms other actors employ when they're called upon to play a retarded or handicapped person. He makes Tim believably retarded through stripping away rather than adding. We get the idea that this is what Mel was like as a child — simple, curious, essentially happy. His dependence on Mary Horton comes naturally. Between Piper Laurie and Mel Gibson there is a sweet warmth, a sympathy that grows as their relationship does. It's fragile but resilient, an unlikely but finally plausible match.

Michael Pate was pleased with their partnership. "In the scene on the beach, I suggested he run alongside Piper and then around her, like a puppy dog. He did a marvellous forward and backward run around her. It was just adorable, the way they worked together."

Piper Laurie also remembers their working

relationship fondly. "I'd say he was shy, essentially, but he wasn't shy with me. We laughed and joked and had fun a lot." She feels that kind of rapport is important. "There's a 'kid' side of me, a really silly, giggly side of me, and I find that indulging it is very useful when I'm working on things that are very intense. It almost saves me. So I loved Mel's silliness and his humour."

The first time we as an audience — and Mary as a character — really begin to care for Tim is the moment early in the film when she's conscientiously given him a break from gardening and a cup of tea (there do seem to be endless cups of tea in this movie). He tells her that he's not "normal," and we see her mind working: that's why he came across as a little overfamiliar; he just doesn't know better. Her cold reserve begins to melt: she's no longer threatened, but feels a wave of maternal concern. Tim finished his tea, stands up and announces disarmingly, "I like you." Then he proceeds to hop across the lawn. Mary is caught by surprise and laughs spontaneously. You have a feeling that she hasn't laughed in a long time. Tim is pleased.

"That was my special imitation of a kangaroo," he says proudly. Mary smiles and says, "I could tell right away."

From then on, her feelings for him deepen steadily, until she has to admit to herself that it is more than maternal interest or even friendship. She's fallen in love. This realization frightens her, but she cares more about Tim than about herself and puts her fears aside in order to protect him.

The film becomes especially interesting to watch as

the actors are challenged by the story's melodramatic turn of events. The cast comes through with their good taste intact. Mel's firm grounding in the character allows him to experience truthful responses to every stimulus without having to manufacture or map them out ahead of time. It's something he and many good actors can do; it makes the difference between mediocrity and a superior performance.

Acting is really, as legendary teacher Sanford Meisner said, not "acting" at all, but *doing*. It's responding to what hits you, the way you respond in real life. The stoplight turns green, you go. The coffee burns your tongue, you spit it out. The tennis ball comes your way, you hit it back. When you can, as Meisner puts it, "*do* truthfully under imaginary circumstances" then you can call yourself an actor.

Tim was released in Australia in 1978. The combination of an interesting situation, a low-key, literate script and a collection of original and capable performances made *Tim* a success. Mel Gibson's own opinion of the project is, in retrospect, realistic. "It was interesting but not terribly complicated," he says. "There are good and bad things about the film. It's got a lot of rough edges, but I think it's made with a lot of heart."

According to Piper Laurie, what we see on film is only a third of how effective it *could* have been. "I think a lot was wasted in rehearsal, and that's a fault of the director. As good as Mel was, he would have been just absolutely brilliant."

Although some critics faulted the film's simplistic approach and called it oversentimental, they all praised its acting. *The New York Times* wrote, "Considering the patent silliness of the material. Miss Laurie and Mr. Gibson do very well, and the supporting players, especially Mr. Kurts, are fine.''

At the Australian Film Institute Awards in 1979 (Australia's equivalent to the Oscars) both Alwyn Kurts and Pat Evison won Best Supporting Actor Awards for *Tim*, and Mel Gibson won the coveted Best Actor Award for his performance in the title role.

CHAPTER

7

ATTACK FORCE Z

In early 1980, Mel was cast in a film called *Attack Force Z,* a World War II action adventure about an Australian Green-beret-type special forces unit that conducted secret operations in the West Pacific. The film stars American actor John Phillip Law, with Mel Gibson as Captain Paul Kelly, leader of a mission to liberate a Pacific island occupied by the Japanese. The cast also includes the highly-respected New Zealand actor, Sam Neill, who made his name in Gillian Armstrong's *My Brilliant Career* and Australians Chris Haywood and John Waters.

The film was beset with conceptual difficulties from pre-production. Realistically, location shooting should have been set in South East Asia, on an island off Indonesia or New Guinea where the exploits of the Australian war-time commandoes actually took place. But the Australian producers, John MacCallum and Lee Robinson, had set up their co-production with the Taiwanese, so the location was transposed to North East Asia, which introduced a number of credibility problems. For instance, the place-names and currency were Dutch — suggesting the Dutch East Indies, but the population and culture were clearly Chinese.

The Australian producers had worked before on an action adventure TV series in Malaya, and were obviously attracted to the exotic locations, cheap labour, low-cost local cast and crew to be found in the East. But troubles soon began to emerge between the co-production partners. Cultural differences, Taiwanese film-making customs and methods of getting things done varied greatly from the West, as Francis Ford Coppola found when he created the hell of the Vietnam War in the Philippines a few years earlier. *Attack Force Z* was to have the lot.

Moreover, AFI award winner Philip Noyce, who had made his reputation directing and engaging, if overly political and parochial docu-drama film, *Newsfront,* wanted to give the script, written by Englishman Roger Marshall from an idea by producer Robinson, a more political angle putting greater emphasis on the theme of the local population's resistance and final uprising against Japanese occupation forces. For box-office reasons, the producers were anxious to preserve the action/adventure nature of the film.

Another problem in the joint Aussie/Taiwanese production was the star-status of the American, John Phillip Law, who was to be paid $50,000, ten times more than either Sam Neill or Mel Gibson who were on a paltry $1000 a week. They had been persuaded to work on the film by Noyce for much less than their usual fees, on the understanding that he would be controlling the script.

John Phillip Law had been cast by the producers, not by Noyce, and his "star" status looked shaky compared to Neill and Mel fresh from their successes with *My Brilliant Career* and *Mad Max.*

It created tensions that under some circumstances could be constructive in a movie where stars were pitted against each other, but not in this one. Added to this was the fact that the crew were Chinese and none of them spoke English. There was just one interpreter and he was working overtime during rehearsals.

The producers demanded that Noyce get the production started, but he filibusted, saying the script was not yet ready to shoot. The producers answered that he had had nine weeks in pre-production. They couldn't afford to extend it any further. It was soon a case of, did he jump or was he pushed? Noyce left Taiwan. The $800,000 production (half each put up by Australia and Taiwan), was in danger of folding.

The Australian Film Commission, which had supported *Attack Force Z,* rang Melbourne-based director Tim Burstall, an important figure in Australia's film industry renaissance, who just completed the epic, *Eliza Fraser,* and the action drama, *The Last of the Knucklemen.*

"Can you get on a plane in ten hours?" was the first question he was asked by the AFC. When he answered in the affirmative he was told he had to be ready to start directing within hours of getting off the plane. Burstall asked to see all the scripts which he picked up from producer John MacCallum in Sydney en route to Taiwan. Burstall read the scripts on the plane and decided to base it on the original version.

The new director arrived to find the "worst film mess" he had ever encountered. The Chinese were suspicious of the Australians, sensing dissent in the camp. Ko Ching Chang, the Chinese star, thought the film would fold. John Phillip Law whose allegiance was to the producers, was "frankly relieved" to see Noyce go, but had no knowledge of Burstall as a producer.

The Australian leads were ringing their agents, trying to get off the picture. The crew were confused and according to Taiwanese journalist, Kim Lun Chow, who wrote a story on the production for the Far Eastern Economic Review, "there was much tension and negativity, especially from the Australians."

"The cast naturally had residual loyalty to Noyce and Burstall had the unenviable tasks of pulling the cast and crew together and engendering a positive attitude," Lun

Chow reported. "During the ridiculously short time of rehearsal under Burstall's direction, the Australians seemed to be refusing to cooperate. He stopped rehearsing and took the cast out of earshot of the Taiwanese and others, and had words with them. The Australians then went back to work, at last making an effort."

Burstall recalls it another way.

"There wasn't any dramatic confrontation," he says, "but when I arrived everyone was understandably demoralised. I had to appeal to their professionalism to get things underway. Mel, Sam and Chris (Haywood) responded well and we were able to make a start."

According to Lun Chow, it was Sam Neill who initially expressed confidence in Burstall, having liked Burstall's *The Last of the Knucklemen*. "Neill told Mel Gibson and the others he thought Burstall could handle the film and that settled everyone down."

Ko Ching Chang, who Lun Chow called "the Marlon Brando of the East", summoned Burstall to a meeting the moment he arrived and the two men, communicating through an interpreter, immediately hit it off.

However, when shooting began there was an incident, which again threatened the production.

"As everything was shot non-sequentially," Lun Chow reported, "early on no one seemed sure of where Burstall was taking the movie. In an action sequence, the director was conferring with his stunt co-ordinator — a Taiwanese who had no English. As Burstall explained the stunt choreography to the cast, Gibson became convinced that he was being robbed of the dramatic initiative, and he accused the director of giving Ko Ching Chang too much of the scene. He threw down his submachine gun and stomped off the set. Burstall had to call for a break to explain things to, and placate, an extremely mad Mel. In the end the director convinced Mel that he had it wrong. The climax of the scene was all Mel's."

Burstall had little opportunity of shooting the script in sequence, especially as the opening needed a submarine. It had to be filmed at Jarvis Bay in Australia. The director decided on an unusual ploy by flying in Australian actor John Waters to start the movie and then killing him off early for stunning and dramatic effect.

The director had to re-work the script with Robinson each night and there were continual problems, such as the lack of a certain type of plane mentioned in a scene. It had to be written out. Burstall went for scenes that exploited the local landscape. Temples and villages were used.

Lun Chow was critical. "Monks were aghast at the violence surrounding their temples and sacred ground," he commented, "and they more than once complained about the violent scenes going on in their vicinity."

However, the action scenes seemed to release some of the tension which pervaded in the early days. Mel in particular seemed to rise to the occasion with relish.

"I'd never worked with Mel Gibson," Burstall said, reflecting on the shoot, "but I had admired his work at NIDA and his performance in *Mad Max*. For such a physical actor, he has great sensitivity. He has an unusual dynamism, rather like a thoroughbred race horse with a lot of spirit.'

The film (with its 127 killings in ninety-two minutes), miraculously ended in harmony with Ko Ching Chang generously inviting Burstall and the cast to his Japanese restaurant in Kaohsiung. They were surprised to find that each course was accompanied by a fresh group of young geisha girls who, according to Lun Chow, "helped the guests with their digestion".

The final edited result of *Attack Force Z* was not the turkey or failure that many expected, but a yeoman-like production considering its limitations. While the actual production values were criticised by reviewers, Burstall's direction and the performances of Law, Gibson, Neill and the stunning Sylvia Chang, plus the taut editing of David Stiven, all received fair, sometimes fullsome reviews, Every so often the actors rose above the workmanlike yet patchy script and made moments genuinely exciting. Mel was as intense and emotionally honest as ever. He did nothing when nothing was called for and put across the intentions of the story intelligently.

The film went on release in seventy-three countries and in the end did Mel's reputation no harm. Even today it stands up reasonably well in TV repeats. After the film was made, Burstall remarked that he would be "amazed if Mel isn't in Hollywood in the next twelve months. All he has to do is change a few vowels."

Vowels apart, that prediction proved accurate, but not before the actor embarked on a story about the fortunes of war, called *Gallipoli,* which was to give him a sound base for his launch into the bigtime.

An even sounder base for the meteoric rise to come was meeting his wife. In late 1979, a friend told him about a girl he had met at a dating agency, and urged Mel to join it. The *Mad Max* phenomenon had given Mel a minor cult following in Australia, and as he was to discover later, throughout the world and he was beginning to comprehend what being a "star" at large could mean.

For a start, it reduced one's privacy to zero. In the local supermarket, chemist and pubs, he was becoming a face people recognized. He had no trouble meeting women, but they weren't always the *right* women. And with the star image emerging, it didn't seem quite appropriate for him to be hanging round dances with the boys aiming to get laid. It was becoming too strange and bizarre. With all the hype about his looks and charm there was another point: Mel was basically shy with the opposite sex. He was nervous, sometimes tongue-tied and never relaxed. The chase business exhausted him. Deep-down he longed for stability. Even in his early twenties he often told friends about his looking forward to a more settled existence.

The privacy of a dating agency seemed appealing and apt on many levels. It was discrete and without the role-playing and time-wasting. The parties were not, unless they were being frivolous, after mere sexual encounters. They desired a partner, preferably for life. Presumably a good agency would put together suitable individuals, which seemed eminently sensible.

Any long term relationship for Mel was going to mean a checklist for the chosen female. Right on top would be ''Catholic'' and ''desire for a big family.'' Mel Gibson wanted to breed. He had come from a home with lots of kids. He enjoyed the small-tribe environment and huge love involved with large numbers. Any future partner would need to have the same attitude and desires.

In a sense Mel was wanting to ''get on with it'' too. His father had always told him that if he wanted a big, happy family he should start young because it would be demanding.

''Marrying and having kids will help settle you down,''

Hutton often told Mel, "then you can get on with your life — your work — with greater maturity."

The woman with the most in common with him was a dark-haired, Sydney nurse called Robyn Moore. She was five feet six inches tall with big, dark brown eyes and high-cheekbones. She was a no-nonsense woman who wanted to become friends before any thoughts of romance. Mel immediately felt comfortable with her. She put him at ease in a way that had rarely happened. They got to know each other very well before their relationship suddenly blossomed. By mid-1980, Mel was thinking seriously about marriage.

"I had never been so nervous in my life," he said later. "And I don't think I ever actually *proposed*. I sort of fumbled out a question. I sort of *asked*. It was the toughest thing. I choked more than once."

Fortunately, Robyn was willing.

In Sydney, in August 1980, Mel met with several actor friends, including Chris Haywood, in a bar. After a drink or two, one of them suggested they move on to a nightclub. Mel surprised the little group by opting out. He had a girlfriend called Robyn, whom he had decided to marry.

"My playing days are over," he told the group. "No more wild women and partying. I'm going to be a family man."

There was a strange silence as they wondered if Mel, always the court jester, was joking. But he wasn't. According to one of the actors with him that night, his demeanour was "firm and relaxed. He had come to a decision and Mel was always good at following through with something once he had made up his mind."

Mel and Robyn married in October 1980.

Theirs seems to be one of those rare phenomena — not just in Hollywood but anywhere — a solid, successful marriage. It's also very, very private. In the face of almost unbelievable pressure from the press to reveal his every personal secret, Mel Gibson has kept his wife and family shielded from public exposure. It's not easy nor is it a pleasant problem to have to deal with every day. "Being a star is being a target," he says. "It's like having your pants down around your ankles and your hands tied behind your back."

To be as tremendously popular a public figure as Gibson has become is also a Catch-22, because he's popular for the very reasons (lack of ego, down-to-earth attitude), that sometimes makes him wish he weren't. And it's not an idle, wistful desire, either. It's an active, passionate one. Mel Gibson reportedly once told director Roger Spottiswoode in a moment of social candour that he wished he could die and come back to life as somebody no one knew. It's understandable. The trade-off is clear. You make millions of dollars doing something that you love and that's your life's work, and people enjoy it. That's the good part. Then you can't turn around, eat dinner in a restaurant or take your kids to a ball game like a normal father without getting a flashbulb in the face or being asked a rude question. That's the bad.

It's not a new problem, of course. Since fame became a matter of public consumption by cinematic and electronic means, actors who become stars have also become unreal symbols, victims of their audience's limited attention spans and predictable assumptions. Imagine how it must feel for an intelligent person, sitting down to read a magazine, to discover in its pages some stranger's total misrepresentation of his life, work and relationships. It's almost as if the public needs to punish you for giving them what they so desperately seem to want.

What is known by everyone who knows Mel Gibson is that his priority is — just as it was for his dad — his family. He brings his wife and children (now six and counting), with him everywhere he can. They are his anchor. He depends on them for his sanity. He says, "Life's not life without them."

When Mel Gibson married Robyn Moore in 1980, indications were already very good that he'd have a rewarding career as a working actor. But it must have been impossible for either of them to guess at the magnitude of Mel's eventual success. It was to happen very quickly, even for the mercurial world of showbusiness, and it's a testament to their devotion to each other and to their individual strengths that they have come through the firestorm of rapid celebrity with their private life intact.

CHAPTER

8

THE ECHO OF SCREAMS

"You know Frank. He'd sell his own grandmother for tuppence, and still talk his way into heaven."

Bert in *Gallipoli*

The Australian word *larrikin* means a scalliwag, a mischievous youth who isn't quite a scoundrel, but who just might go wrong if badly influenced. He's got a twinkle in his eye and a grin for the ladies. There's not much he takes seriously aside from his own well-being. He's sort of Australian archetype, the kind of boy a girl might be reckless enough to dance with but would be foolish to marry.

This description would apply pretty accurately to Mel Gibson's character, Frank Dunne, in Peter Weir's stunning and evocative 1981 film, *Gallipoli*. At least it describes the larrikin Frank we meet at the film's beginning. Unable even to ride a horse properly, he manages to talk his way into the glamorous Light Horse Regiment, strutting for his envious mates in his new cocked hat and eliciting the comment above from one of them.

By film's end, he's undergone a change so profound that on a personal level his transformation parallels the entire meaning of the film. It becomes historical allegory.

The World War I Battle of Gallipoli is as well-known in Australian history as Waterloo is to the English or Gettysburg to Americans. Its emotional meaning to the Australian national identity is difficult to overestimate; it remains an event surrounded by an aura of almost surreal tragedy, and it is for all Australians a rich source of pride.

The year was 1915. Turkey had entered the war on the side of the Central Powers the previous October, creating a geographical barrier between Russia to the east and the rest of the Allies to the west. This made it nearly impossible to get supplies through to Russia, which was being badly battered by German forces, so something had to be done. A costly naval attack having failed, 75,000 English, Australian, New Zealand and French troops tried to open a new front at a point at the mouth of the Bosphorus called the Gallipoli Peninsula, a narrow cape extending between the Aegean Sea to the west and the Dardanelles to the east. Their goal was to gain control of the Dardanelles, the Bosphorus Straits and Constantinople (now Istanbul), thus opening Black Sea supply routes to Russia.

According to what has become legend, the British commanders and their Australian counterparts failed to synchronize timepieces accurately (in the film, it's two Australian watches against one English one, implicating the British officer as carelessly arrogant). The planned attack against their entrenched enemy, the Turks, was to be a twofold one: first British artillery would knock out Turkish emplacements, then infantry, Australian and New Zealander, would immediately attack and finish the job. What actually happened was a result of tragic miscalculation combined with a breakdown of field communications and it ended in the unnecessary deaths of thousands of Australian troops.

The Australian sergeant major whose responsibility it was to order the charge from the trenches had a nearly impossible decision to make. He was ordered to charge at a specified time, but the preparatory artillery barrage had begun earlier than expected, and ceased ten minutes too soon, according to his watch. His troops waited for orders while he phoned to headquarters to see if there was a final burst of artillery fire planned. In the short interim, Turkish troops poured back into their own trenches, making their defence nearly impenetrable.

In the film, Major Barton, played beautifully by Bill Hunter, begging his British superior to fire more artillery, says, "Do you realise they're back in the trenches, sir?" The Englishman is implacable, and insists that the Australian troops attack according to plan. They do, and meet with disaster. Three waves of infantry come screaming out of the trenches toward the Turks and are mowed down like dry wheat.

Meanwhile, Major Barton has sent a runner, Frank Dunne, to headquarters to explain the situation as field communications have broken down. Frank finally gets the word from the British officer in charge that the assault should be halted, but despite his desperate attempt to return with the news in time, the order to attack is given, and his best mate Archy is killed in the charge as Frank screams in anguish.

Gallipoli was the inspiration of director Peter Weir, who was in 1981 one of the brightest rising stars in the Australian film firmament, after successes throughout the 'seventies with films like *The Cars That Ate Paris, Picnic at Hanging Rock* and *The Last Wave.* Weir had long been fascinated by the story of Gallipoli and had made a pilgrimage there in 1976. Alone on the site of the battlefield for two days, he explored it, finding relics like army buttons and pieces of leather belts still left there from the battle over sixty years before.

"I felt somehow I was really touching history," he remembers. "It totally altered my perception of Gallipoli." The experience convinced him that he needed to make the film.

One of Weir's primary objectives was verisimilitude, which for a period film requires months of preparation, research, painstaking attention to detail — and, most important, working with the right people. There's a certain passion some theatre and film artists have about history, a love for the idea of going back in time, that comes through their work. It shows in the films of Merchant/Ivory, John Huston or David Lean. It's not as simple as recreating what we imagine was historical reality; it's also an attitude, a little extra silver in the mirror they're holding up to time.

Peter Weir chose his team carefully for *Gallipoli*. David Williamson was the screenwriter with whom he worked from the beginning. Williamson, a respected playwright who went on to successful career in film, was known for his social and political perceptiveness as well as for his sensitivity to atmosphere and knowledge of historical framework. Together, they created the fictional friendship of two Australian boys to dramatise in an intimate, personal way the greater event that was their subject.

"Our first approach," says Weir, "was to tell the whole story from enlistment in 1914 through to the evacuation of Gallipoli at the end of 1915, but we were not getting at what this thing was, the burning centre that had made Gallipoli a legend. I could never find the answers in any books, and it certainly wasn't evolving in any of our drafts, so we put the legend to one side and simply made up a story about two young men, really got to know them, where they came from, what happened to them along the way, spent more time getting to the battle and less time on the battlefield."

The director of photography was the brilliant Russell Boyd, whose compositions of light and shadows had helped make Weir's *Picnic at Hanging Rock* so affecting.

Boyd took the landscapes of Western and South Australia and made poetry with them, filling their empty spaces with light, and making them act almost as a third character witnessing the growing friendship of Frank and Archy. The scene in the vast empty salt lake that Archy and Frank have to cross on their journey to Perth to join the army is especially remarkable. The scene begins at ground level, the camera following the two as they trudge toward the horizon's vanishing point. Then the camera sweeps up and out, catching their tiny, lonely figures making slow progress across the expanse of white sand as the desert wind howls around them.

Later, the evening before battle, while Major Barton listens in his tent to a haunting duet from Bizet's *The Pearl Fishers,* we see the Australian encampment's lanterns twinkling on the shore and the lights of a Red Cross ship gently bobbing as shells burst in the distance.

Every aspect of the film was meticulously researched. Historical experts, including military advisers, were engaged to ensure authenticity in every detail. With an extraordinary level of attention the thousands of extras who played Australian, New Zealander and British soldiers were given printed notes with historical information pertaining to that day's shoot, so they would feel more in tune with what had actually occurred.

The look of the film was inextricably connected to its message, in that the images the audience saw on the screen were responsible for carrying the weight of the legend. As author Brian McFarlane explains in his book *Australian Cinema,* "Everyone who sees Peter Weir's *Gallipoli* will *receive* exactly the same visual image even if everyone may *perceive* it differently: the mediation of director, writer, actors and cameraman has had its way with the image before the viewer sees it — the film's image, through its representation of the actual, stands a better chance of being received as myth distilled.''

A significant part of that image was, of course, the look of the actors. Peter Weir had seen Mel Gibson in *Mad Max* and felt strongly about his physical as well as his emotional qualities on film. *Gallipoli*'s producer, Pat Lovell, had given Mel a copy of the screenplay's first draft and asked him to look at the part of Frank. After a screen test, he was hired on the spot. "He was like a rough-cut diamond," Weir remembers. "That charisma — it's even there in his baby photographs." As a contrast to Mel's dark, rougher look, they cast Mark Lee, whose fairness puts across a sunny, innocent purity, as Arch. The two actors, opposites in manners, personalities and physical appearance, represent the two Australias that were waging an ideological war with each other while the world beyond its borders fought a military one.

Archy is the old Australia. He behaves himself, pushes himself to do his best with honour, believes in the British Empire and in tradition. Frank is the new Australia, opportunistic and iconoclastic, scoffing at the thought of giving up his life for a country not his own. "It's not our bloody war," he says. "It's an English war." But this is an understandable expression of baffled resentment at the situation. Most Australians, intensely loyal to flag and empire, were happy and proud to enlist. It was *their* war too and however tragically the Gallipoli episode concluded, Australians, then, were fervent in their desire to vanquish the common enemy.

Early in the film, as we are getting to know both

characters, we see in the golden lamplight Arch's Uncle Jack reading to the children from Kipling's *The Jungle Book:*

> Then something began to hurt Mowgli inside him, as he'd never been hurt in his life before. And he caught his breath and sobbed, and the tears ran down his face. "What is it? What is it?" he said. "I do not wish to leave the jungle. And I do not know what this is. Am I dying Bagheera?" "No, little Brother," said Bagheera. "Those are only tears, such as men use. Now I know thou art a man, and a man's cub no longer. Let them fall, Mowgli. They're only tears." So Mowgli sat and cried as though his heart would break. And he'd never cried in all his life before.

The choice is a telling one, not only because Kipling was one of Britain's foremost literary representatives of the golden age of the empire, but also because this passage foreshadows the breaking of illusions and the encroachment of the outside world. What's ironic is that it turns out to be the cynical Frank whose preconceptions are shattered, not those of the idealistic Archy, as we had expected.

These two characters, appropriately, begin as opponents. Their race against each other ends with Arch's victory and Frank's sullen admission of defeat. But soon they make friends (partly because Frank's lack of funds encourages him to be more sociable) and decide to enlist together. Their reasons are disparate but their needs are equally acute. Frank needs food, shelter and a job, and Arch needs to fight for a cause.

From then on, they are "mates," and this is one of the major themes of the film. Even early on, before Archy meets Frank, he's challenged by a neighbourhood villain because he's being friendly with his family's Aboriginal servant. He stands straight and, eyes flashing, announces, "Zak and I are mates." To be a mate is a sacred obligation in Australia, the land of male-dominated loyalties. When Archy and Frank become mates, it's the strongest most powerful relationship the film offers and its strength gives the ending of the story a terrible impact.

Mel Gibson gives a superb performance in *Gallipoli*. He's thoroughly relaxed, but that doesn't mean he's slack or casual. Relaxation for an actor means not being tense and anxious, allowing the meaning of what you're doing to flow through you so you can experience it — and communicate it — fully. If an actor can achieve real relaxation, his body can do its interpretive job.

He's also completely at home. He allows himself to sink into the situation, without questioning or watching himself doing it. This ability to believe the imaginary circumstances around you without working at it is sometimes called "actor's faith." It's very similar to what children do when they throw themselves into a backyard "Let's Pretend" scenario — they just do it, with no questions asked.

In *Gallipoli,* Mel Gibson is doing it because it's fun. His enjoyment of the work is obvious. For an actor, there's no more satisfying feeling than riding the crest of a wave of imagination, with a team of intelligent, passionate people behind you, and finding the most that the story and its meaning can offer to an audience. It's a better high than any drug has ever been able to provide.

But the sheer work it takes to achieve this level of creativity is grueling. On locations like *Gallipoli's* (Western and South Australia and Egypt), the crew and actors were pushed to their limit. Everyone, regardless of stature or job title, worked together. Mel Gibson lugged camera equipment to the top of a pyramid. After filming the empty salt lake scene in South Australia's dried out Lake Torrens for days, the company was appalled to learn that they'd all been walking and crawling around among deadly funnelweb spiders. In Cairo everyone came down with a strange stomach bug but they kept on shooting. There were dust storms and hot winds, endless night shoots in small, damp boats that slammed against the waves to the accompaniment of a freezing wind. Shooting went on in the trenches despite the grains of sand that blew into everyone's eyes. Toward the end of the film, Mel Gibson contracted glandular fever but he kept going.

Under the best of conditions, making a film is rarely easy. For everyone connected with *Gallipoli,* it was an incredible physical achievement.

And for Mel, it was a highly emotional time as well. Robyn was pregnant with their first child, and they'd known that the baby would come while he was on location. He experienced the birth with her, at long distance on the phone from Egypt, tears running down his face. It was a girl. They named her Hannah.

Gallipoli, with its magnificent cinematography, inspired direction, spare and intelligent screenplay, an eloquent score (Albinoni's Adagio in G Minor during the battle scenes) and top-flight performances, was a phenomenal artistic success. Reviews were uniformly favourable and Mel Gibson drew raves. *The New York*

Times called him an overnight sensation, and praised his "wit, ingenuity and range." Executive producers Robert Stigwood and Rupert Murdoch had a solid hit their first time out and *Gallipoli's* worldwide showing pleased its distributor, Paramount.

It was a bit of a surprise, however. "We suddenly realised we were dealing with a phenomenon," one senior Vice President of marketing recalls. "Here we are, [at a time] when major films are not opening, and in comes a film made in Australia with no presence in America and on word-of-mouth alone does great business." To accommodate its enthusiastic audiences, one New York cinema had a twenty-four-hour nonstop schedule of screenings. But in spite of artistic and urban box office success, in the U.S. the film grossed only a little over $12.5 million; not a disaster, by any means, but disappointing given its mainstream release. The film was the first Australian import to have been widely released commercially in North America — *Breaker Morant* and *My Brilliant Career* were essentially art-house movies — and, its artistic merit notwithstanding, *Gallipoli* remained inaccessible to most of North America.

"It is very easy to be wise in retrospect, but *Gallipoli,* I don't feel, should have been called *Gallipoli* outside Australia," says producer Pat Lovell. "In America, they said, 'What's Gallipoli? Some new kind of spaghetti?' I think it was probably wrong to put it out worldwide under that title, and I do think that, especially theatrically, it suffered a little."

Whatever the fate of the film (it has been one of Paramount Home Video's best-sellers) and it was a gigantic boost upward for one of its stars. Mel Gibson, in a class act,

had arrived on America's shores, and many were in love
with him. Some people were also enamoured of Australian
films in general, which paved the way for Gibson's next
and Australia's first great U.S. success, an entirely different
story, a sequel to *Mad Max* called *The Road Warrior*.

CHAPTER

9

MAX RETURNS

"Films are like public dreams: we go to dark places and sit with strangers to watch something up on the screen that ultimately comes from the collective unconsciousness."

George Miller

Mad Max 2, or *The Road Warrior,* is a fun movie. Pure summertime, sci-fi easy-to-watch fun. It has substance, humour, lots of suspense, violence, emotion, a kid and a dog. But most of all, it has Max.

Since we saw Max last, the world has been decimated by a cataclysmic nuclear holocaust precipitated by two warrior tribes. The remains of civilization are now scavengers for the precious fuel that rules their existence. Max is riding the highways, looking, like everybody else, for a few drops of gasoline to keep him going.

Mel Gibson's take on Max in *The Road Warrior* is absorbing to watch because he's been tempered by time, experience and the chance to see the character with the perspective of hindsight. This Max is broader and deeper, stronger and smarter. He's still amazingly good looking, but his face has been marked by tragedy. His illusions have been broken.

The elements that make up the sequel to *Mad Max* were carefully assembled. The George Miller/Byron Kennedy partnership, begun ten years earlier, had achieved the first *Max* on a shoestring budget. Now they had ten times as much money, a witty script by Miller, Terry Hayes and Brian Hannant, an even more eclectic cast of characters and a wild and crazy collection of stuntpeople, many of whom were, in fact, recruits from the demolition derby circuit. In Australia these are called "auto crack shows."

Miller and Kennedy had learned a lot from their first time around. They were tireless in their quest for perfection, and although Miller had come to film direction late, after a career as a doctor, he had boundless energy, imagination and dedication. These characteristics combined with experience and an original, passionate vision turned Miller into the genius many industry people describe him as today.

As for producer Byron Kennedy, he was considered to be a genius at marketing, partly because he spent much of his time and effort learning as much as he could about his audiences. In the corporate world, if a company makes a product and wants to gauge its success, it hires a market research specialist to conduct controlled consumer-response sessions called focus groups, where real consumers tell you exactly what they think about the product. In film-making, they've become much more sophisticated; you stand in the back of the theatre and listen. So Kennedy travelled around the world after *Mad Max* opened, monitoring audience reactions in Japan, France, Spain and England. He and George Miller had a habit of interviewing the journalists who were trying to interview them, to find out what *they* thought about the film and how it might have been improved. They analized, brainstormed and asked a million questions. A Warner Brothers executive, John Friedkin, emphasized the significance of their approach. "A lot of people in this business, after a hit, think they know everything; they don't ask, all of a sudden they pontificate. Not Byron and George; these are two very bright young guys still wanting to *learn,* and it is heartening to see — and more heartening because it is working for them."

Their larger budget made a big difference. Now *Mad Max* could travel to a real location. For the first film, they'd had to shoot just a few miles away from a major city. It had been difficult to avoid trees, telephone lines and other jarring reminders of civilization. This time, they could afford to travel with an enormous cast and crew into the heartland of Australia, a vast, empty landscape. Like most location shoots, it wasn't easy, but at least they could pay for it. They had a tough act to follow when it came to stunts, so they spent a great deal of preproduction time planning even more elaborate ones and putting together a team of experienced professionals to work with their car-cracking specialists. Fortunately, they could now produce more precise (and expensive), sound effects to enhance each explosion and high-speed collision.

In *Road Warrior* the camera technique was crucial. If you look for it, you can see that the camera never takes a passive point of view, watching the action go by. Instead, it's mobile, like the characters. "The camera must be a participant," said Byron Kennedy. "That's our basic, underlying philosophy, so that the audience can participate rather than observe." It is the classic purpose of the tracking shot.

Another technical achievement in *Road Warrior,* and part of what makes it work, is the editing. "I haven't seen anyone else slice a picture up in quite that way," says Mel Gibson. "He knew exactly what he wanted to do with it before he did it, so it's pure film craft." the final product is deceptively simple and easy to watch, but what went into it was hours of painstaking calculation about the number of seconds for each shot and sequence, how one frame reacts against another, how the audience will respond in terms of surprise and suspense. These last two elements are a speciality of Miller's, who finds inspiration in the work of legendary director Alfred Hitchcock: "Hitchcock said it best when he said that surprise is when you don't expect something to happen and it does, and suspense is when you expect something to happen and it doesn't."

The moment in *Road Warrior* when Wez pops up in front of the truck is a good example of cinematic surprise, and it works every time — even if you've already seen the film. The timing is just so surprising that you don't expect it to happen. In a cinema, the entire audience jumps. Miller accomplished it with a kind of double switch; you think that the Feral Kid, who is crawling out on the hood of the truck to get the last bullet for Max, is about to fall. Will he grab the bullet? Will he be able to hold on? That's what you're waiting for. Then Miller surprises you with danger from a startling angle. As Mel Gibson puts it, "It's a total freak-out."

There's also a kind of science fiction elegance about *Road Warrior* that its predecessor didn't possess. Miller and Kennedy were careful to give immediate hints about the specifics of the film's genre, so we can sit back and enjoy what we're seeing. There's no confusion. This is the same reason for the huge sucess of *Star Wars;* from the beginning of the film you're locked into its style. It allows you to suspend disbelief and enjoy the adventure. In other words, the filmmakers have said, "This is going to be fun; don't over-analize it, just get into it. Trust us; you'll have a great time."

And like the best science fiction and the best of any genre, really, the most horrific, graphically violent moments are left to the audience's imagination. This, of course, gives them much more impact. Even in *Mad Max,* Miller was aware of this technique and used it effectively. "If you look at the film piece by piece, you would see very, very little blood. It's so much more powerful that way. One thing I learned very quickly was to keep the monster out of the screen, as it were; that nothing is so strong as the audience's projected unconscious on to what is happening.''

There is also, in *Road Warrior*, a cockeyed sense of humour that takes the darkness of the concept and shines a ray of light through it. Bruce Spence, as the Gyro Captain, makes the best of his character's comic personna. He cuts through pretension and says the lines with perfect wistfulness: ''Remember desserts? Lawn chairs? Remember *lingerie?*'' He's a refreshing contrast to Max's solemnity and every once in a while he even goads Max into a smile or two. He's open where Max is closed and voluable where Max is silent. His contretemps with Max's dog over the remains of a can of dog food manages to be funny rather than depressing. His presence in the film defines the phrase ''comic relief.''

The Road Warrior's visual style is wittily outrageous. Its costumes are punk, drag and leather-studded for the villains and light, natural and voluminous for the good guys. Norma Moriceau, the costume designer, calls her wasteland costumes ''Male Trouble, Big Butch Business''. It's all to do with ''male sports and the medals men give each other in clubs and things.'' She used football pads, hockey masks (predating Freddy) and horsehair tails, with accessories like bike reflectors, rear view mirrors and metal automotive logos.

Weapons are an amalgam of medieval crossbows, shotguns and deadly Asian darts, with double-bladed harpoons and a mace thrown in for good measure. Vehicles range from souped-up hot cars, jalopies, eighteen-wheelers and an armoured school bus to bizarre Buck

Rogers chariots and a mosquito-like gyrocopter. It's a three-ring stylistic circus; its acrobats, jugglers and clowns are characters with names like Humungus, Wez, Pappagalo, Gyro Captain and the Feral Kid. The one character without a creative name is the only one who would normally have one: Dog.

The original score by Queen guitarist Brian May — romantic one minute and appropriately epic the next — pumps heart-thumping excitement into every frame. It provides a solid sensual foundation for the sound track and for the fast-paced editing of the film's special effects.

All of this swirls around Mel Gibson as Max in a crazy, emotion-driven whirlpool that draws him in, in spite of his refusal to become involved. The whole movie is about Max's rescue from a future as empty as the wasteland around him. At the film's end, even though we're unsure of his fate, we know he's been touched by humanity again, and that there is hope.

The voice-over from the grown-up Feral Kid at the beginning of the film has prepared us: "Most of all, I remember the Road Warrior, the man we called Max, a burnt-out, desolate man haunted by the demons of his past. A man who wandered out into the wasteland. And it was here, in this blighted place, that he learned to live again."

Mel Gibson's performance, backed by the care and dedication of Miller, Kennedy and a superb cast, was greeted with exuberance by critics and audiences around the world. He'd understood the necessity for complete restraint, and his powerfully silent presence was what made the rest of the film work. Critics noticed his "unnarcissistic intensity". Charles Michener, in *Newsweek*, said, "His easy, unswaggering masculinity and hint of Down Under humour may be quintessentially Australian but is also the stuff of an international male star." The notoriously critical French press called him "the new John Wayne." Audiences everywhere were captivated.

George Miller, in explaining Mel Gibson's impact on the screen, said, "He has the potential to be one of the great actors. He has a screen presence and a wide range of abilities, but, more than that, he seems to be deeply obsessed with the acting craft. It's a quiet, almost secret thing, but it's unmistakably there."

In this way, Gibson is very much like the breed of movie star that held sway a generation or so before him. Men like Spencer Tracy, Clark Gable, John Wayne and Gregory Peck never discussed their acting technique as more cerebral actors do. Tracy's formula — "say the lines and don't bump into the furniture," accurately describes their approach. But buried beneath their workaday attitude was the treasure of that secret joy in their craft. For actors like them, it needs to stay secret, ot its power will dissipate. Gibson is that kind of actor. He has that unlearnable quality — presence.

The Road Warrior did phenomenal business everywhere it was released. In the United States, it grossed over $23.5 million in 1982 and it made Mel Gibson a recognizable star. He knew it when one day as he was walking along a Manhattan street, a construction worker from a girder yelled down, "Hey, Mel! How ya' doin'!" His first, naïve response was, "Oh, hi. Do I know you?" It's amusing — but sad, too, because Mel Gibson was about to be forced to make the reluctant journey from a normal life

— the sort of life every construction worker has — to a celebrity's life.

CHAPTER

10

CLOUDED BY DESIRE

"You must watch the shadows and not the puppets. In the Wayang, all is clouded by desire — as fire by smoke or a mirror by dust. And through there, the soul is blinded"

Billy Kwan in *The Year of Living Dangerously*

To open his 1982 film, *The Year of Living Dangerously,* Peter Weir chose the sacred Indonesian art of shadow puppets, called the Wayang, an evocative, mysterious and beautiful theatrical experience that chills and touches you at the same time. It feels as if you're suspended in another time; it's like a rhythmic, drug-induced dream and, when it's over, it takes a few hours to recover your 20th-century equilibrium.

You watch the images of the puppets move across the screen like huge, graceful insects in the glow of flickering firelight. Reverberating through the delighted screams of children is the hollow, bell-like music of the *gamelan.* The thick, romantic air is punctuated by the flames of torches and whirling spirals of smoke. The film is informed by the puppet metaphor — puppet dictators, the manipulation of people, strings, wooden and artificial beings controlled by unseen hands.

There are things, Weir is saying, that we do not understand. We may think we grasp them, and then they disappear like shadows. They don't belong to our realm of comprehension. They don't belong to us.

Indonesia is an archipelago of more than 13,500 islands clustered around the equator northwest of the continent of Australia, forming a natural barrier between the Pacific and Indian Oceans. The country's main islands are Sumatra, Java, Borneo and Sulawesi. The sprawling city of Jakarta, the capital, is on the northwest coast of the island of Java.

During the 12th and 14th centuries the islands of Sumatra and Java achieved empires unrivaled in the East. Their culture and wealth were legendary during the Renaissance and became the motivation for the last voyage of Columbus, to what he hoped would be the treasures of an unspoiled but splendid land. Their wealth, was originally based on the spice trade, precious woods, silks and gems.

In more modern times Indonesia was never politically autonomous. Ruled first by the Portuguese in the 1500s and then for three hundred years by the Dutch, Indonesia had been under Western influence for four centuries. Between the two world wars, a movement for independence began, and in 1945, the charismatic leader Sukarno declared Indonesia a free republic. But the country's strategic Southeast Asian location, its large population and its wealth of natural resources made it a target, and by the 1960s, Indonesia was being pulled in opposite directions: toward the West and toward communist control.

As *The Year of Living Dangerously* begins, Sukarno has declared an ideological war on the West, vowing to rid Indonesia of Western influence in one year, a year of "living dangerously" in the effort to free his countrymen from colonial dependence on their western masters. When Australian journalist Guy Hamilton, played by Mel Gibson, arrives on assignment at Jakarta's airport and is waiting to go through customs, the wall before him is hung with a huge banner: Crush British and U.S. Imperialists, it declares. The husky, resonant voice-over of Billy Kwan, played by Linda Hunt, quietly cuts through the airport babble. "You're an enemy here, Hamilton, like all Westerners. President Sukarno tells the West to go to hell, and today Sukarno is the voice of the Third World."

It's an ominous, provocative beginning for a story that takes us through a crucial political event in Indonesia's history while deliciously spinning the tale of a love affair that alters the lives of two people.

The location for the film was Manila in the Philippines. Weir had chosen it because it was similar to Indonesia geographically and architecturally. Things went fairly smoothly until about two weeks before the end of location shooting was scheduled. Then they got scary.

Right-wing religious groups, fearing that the film was imperialist and anti-Moslem, surrounded the set. They followed the crew and cast everywhere. There were death threats, and everyone was assigned a bodyguard. The White House and the CIA began sending instructions. Finally, producer Jim McElroy and Peter Weir decided to bale out and complete the filming in Sydney, for reasons of safety. The transition was accomplished with a minimum of fuss, considering the circumstances. Everyone stayed calm and cooperative. McElroy remembers, "It was a very tense time for both Peter and me. MGM were asking whether they wanted to go on making the picture; we were about halfway through." Getting out was a little tricky, because passports didn't arrive in time and several company members, including Mel Gibson and Sigourney Weaver, missed the plane. They were forced to stay overnight in a hotel near the airport under assumed names. They finally caught another plane the following afternoon.

"Amazingly, it had no evident effect on Mel," recalls McElroy. "He was right back into the character when we restarted. But that is part of his being so centred . . . this was just another part of the job. That shows what sort of guy he is."

There was a silver lining to their having to escape from

Manila, because Robyn was pregnant again and filming in Sydney meant that Mel could be there for the delivery. He was, and it took all night. Robyn gave birth to twin boys, who were named Christian (presciently), and Edward. The next day Mel reported for work on time, which impressed everyone.

There was never any question of Guy Hamilton's being played by another actor. Even before he directed *Gallipoli,* Peter Weir had been working on *The Year of Living Dangerously,* and he had decided on Mel Gibson as soon as he'd seen him. It was a different kind of role from any Mel had played, and it offered diverse challenges.

First of all, Guy Hamilton was older than Gibson himself, who was only twenty-six. That worried Mel a little. Then, the part was not that of an initiator — Hamilton was the central figure the audience relates to, but not the instigator of action. His job in the film is to *react,* which in many ways is more difficult. Mel Gibson is an actor who doesn't spend time and effort telling you what he's thinking. You fill in the gaps yourself. It's the sign of an intelligent actor, who knows that the audience's imagination can create more powerful feelings on its own than emotions you try to show them. As an artist, you should be like a "feather in the wind," responding honestly but not blatantly to the stimuli that come your way. It's a delicate skill, and much more difficult than taking control of the action yourself.

So Mel Gibson was concerned about making Guy Hamilton interesting. "It was complex getting to the character. *He's* not complex: he's almost boring. I wanted to find out what makes a guy do what Guy Hamilton did." He spent time with journalists who'd been in Jakarta, delving into their reasons for being there. He found that they lived on the edge. "These guys courted danger. They were good drinkers," he says, "ratty, fun men who became unethical bastards to get a story. The story was *God*."

In *The Year of Living Dangerously,* Guy Hamilton has been stifled at the news desk in Sydney, and this is the chance he's been waiting for.

But his predecessor hasn't made things easy, and he finds that the crucial doors are closed to him. All he can come up with for his first story is an insubstantial report describing the "precarious tightrope Sukarno is walking between the PKI (communists) and the right-wing military." His editor at home dismisses it as "a travelogue," and Guy is desperately discouraged.

Enter Billy Kwan, a diminutive cameraman with improbable connections. We've seen Billy at the beginning of the film, typing a dossier about Guy Hamilton, and we're suspicious that he's some kind of agent. But he strikes a deal with Guy, getting him an exclusive interview with the head of the PKI, and Guy is thrilled. He places a story about arms being sent to the communists and Sukarno agreeing to their demands — a real scoop that shakes up the political and journalistic community and makes him an instant hero. It also makes other journalists jealous, and that night at the hotel bar, Guy is goaded into a fistfight with an insufferable American reporter, Pete Curtis, played by in true ugly-American fashion by Michael Murphy.

Billy takes Guy under his wing and introduces him to the British attaché, whose attractive assistant is Jill Bryant, played by Sigourney Weaver. Their first encounter is poolside at the hotel, where Guy gallantly loses a race to Jill's pompous boss, earning her amused respect.

Their interest in each other quickens. During their second meeting at a party, Jill criticizes his latest story, calling it melodramatic. "only my opinion," she says. "My flatmate was moved to tears." Guy shoots back, "What does it take to move *you* to tears, eh?" In the silence, the camera moves from one face to the other, absorbing the sexual tension between them. From then on, Guy is the pursuer, while Jill follows her better judgment and, knowing she's due to leave for England in ten days, holds him at arm's distance.

Billy, however, has engineered this love affair and has tricks up his sleeve. He schedules a lunch with Jill and asks her to meet him at Guy's office. When Jill arrives, Billy is nowhere to be seen, but Guy eagerly offers to drive her to Billy's and then asks her to accompany him to an interview. They get soaking wet in a rainstorm. Sitting in Guy's car laughing, they look frankly into each other's eyes for the first time, knowing they're in love.

Afraid to complicate her life, Jill won't take his phone calls. Finally, one night Billy refers to an invitation for a black-tie reception and asks if Guy is planning to go. He grunts, uninterested. Billy says, "Jill will be there." This changes his mind. Guy roots through the bottom of his suitcase to find a dinner jacket slightly the worse for wear and arrives at the reception just before curfew. He strides through the room of formally dressed guests to where Jill is standing, and almost rudely steers her out onto the balcony, where he holds her against the wall and kisses her, leaving her breathless. When she refuses to go with him he just as abruptly turns and leaves the party, getting into his car. He's about to drive away when she runs to him, opens the passenger door and gets in.

Defiantly flaunting the strictly enforced curfew, they crash through a roadblock, drawing fire from automatic weapons as they go, crazy with the exhilaration of their adventure together. Later, watching the house, Billy knows they're making love. His eyes shine with a mixture of satisfaction and envy.

The part of Billy Kwan was originally cast with a male actor from Australia, one who during rehearsals didn't cut it. Desperate to find someone special for this pivotal role, and with a shooting schedule about to begin, Peter Weir agreed to a screen test for Linda Hunt. He was thrilled. "From the moment I saw her," he says, "I knew it was right. I never would have started out looking for a woman, but that makes the character larger-than-life, not bounded by sexuality." This extraordinary gamble was to pay off in spades, given the general mystery and ambiguity of Billy's character. It was an act of bravery on the part of both the director and Linda Hunt.

The film's themes and messages are all articulated by Billy, either in voice-over or dialogue. He explains the shadow puppets to Guy soon after they've met, and in the process he's explaining Java. "You have to understand the Wayang, the sacred shadow play. The puppet master is a priest — that's why they call Sukarno the great puppet master, balancing the left with the right. Their shadows are souls, and the screen in heaven. You must watch the shadows, not the puppets, the right in constant struggle with the left, the forces of light and darkness in endless balance." Billy's face seems to gleam with wisdom as he says, "In the West we want answers for everything; everything is right or wrong, or good or bad. But in the Wayang, no such final conclusions exist."

Linda Hunt gives Billy many layers, makes him a character with secrets and hidden passions. Billy is a benign manipulator, who makes the people for whom he cares into puppets for his own private *Wayang*. When he feels he's been betrayed by one of them, he is devastated. Billy's emotions are at the centre of the movie, and Linda Hunt makes us feel them with him. Though she was apprehensive about playing a man, she accomplished the task with energy, humour and originality. Her Billy Kwan is fascinating, and her achievement was recognised with an Academy Award.

Mel Gibson's Guy Hamilton is brusque and cynical at first, hiding his insecurity in front of the other, more experienced reporters. When he begins to trust Billy, his candour is disarming and his charm takes over. The relationship between Billy and Guy is one of the most enjoyable elements of the film, because it's based on mutual trust. There's also a wry humour, as when Billy says, "We even look alike." When Guy frowns in evident disbelief, Billy goes on, "Really, it's been noticed. We have the same eyes."

The role of Jill Bryant calls for a lovely, sexy elegance, and Sigourney Weaver delivers it. Her early coolness toward Guy gives a twist of suspense to their incipient love affair and works nicely against both Billy's knowning encouragement and Guy's charm. Her anguish when she discovers he will soon be in danger is a sudden, sincere contrast, revealing a sensibility that, until then, we

weren't sure Jill possessed. Her performance matches Mel Gibson's in subtlety, giving them both the credibility demanded by the plot.

This is the first film in which we see a Mel Gibson character fall in love, and he handles it, as he has everything else, truthfully. Because Guy is not self-aware, the pain and desire he feels surprise him. When he finally takes matters into his own hands and pulls Jill onto the balcony to kiss her, it's as satisfying for the audience as it is for the two lovers. Mel Gibson knows how to make an audience care. As writer Stephen Schiff explains, "He can convey a responsive stillness that draws the audience in like a vacuum, so that when he reacts we react with him, instantaneously."

Throughout the story, the theme put across by Billy Kwan and therefore by the film itself, is one of compassion. Billy's mission is to awaken Guy's conscience when he confronts him: "That's what I like about you, Guy. You really don't care, do you? Or maybe you just don't see." Billy is driven to alleviate the misery he sees everywhere around him, and finally his obsession, in the face of greed, opportunism and revolution, kills him.

Weir makes the most of this theme's potential, with vivid images and a haunting sound track. The music was by Maurice Jarre. Like *Gallipoli, The Year of Living Dangerously* is based in history, and again it is Weir's astute grasp of historical atmosphere that makes the movie so enjoyable to watch, along with Russell Boyd's effective camera work and screenwriter David Williamson's sure adaptation of the novel by C. J. Koch. The film was a respected artistic success and it was selected for the official competition at Cannes. Commercially it was less successful, mostly because it was badly distributed in the United States, says MGM's president of production at the time, Freddie Fields. It had opened to favourable response in a small number of theatres, which was a good beginning, but was then "rushed into broad release before word of mouth had a .chance to build," according to Fields. The result was a poorer showing in America than the film deserved. In the United States, it grossed only a little over $8.5 million. It enjoyed critical, if not box-office success in Britain.

But the critics were pleased, especially with Mel Gibson. Vincent Canby, in *The New York Times,* said, "If this film doesn't make an international star of Mel Gibson, nothing will."

By the time it was released, Mel Gibson was filming again; this time as Fletcher Christian in Roger Donaldson's *The Bounty,* with Anthony Hopkins. He took a few days off to join Peter Weir and Jim McElroy at the Cannes Film Festival, where *The Year of Living Dangerously* was in competition. There, he began to realize how major a star he had become, and what it would mean to his personal life.

Suddenly, it was essential for the press to know everything about him. They beseiged him wherever he went, begging everyone who knew him or with whom he'd worked for comments and interviews. Sigourney Weaver answered frankly, "He's the most gorgeous man I've ever met." The quote became an instant rallying cry for more and more of the same.

In Cannes, while having dinner in a restaurant with a party of ten people, Mel was suddenly and violently accosted by a stranger, a French woman, who threw her arms around him and, in the words of Jim McElroy, "stuck her tongue about six inches down his throat. He hadn't requested it. It just came straight out of left field." He managed to extricate himself graciously and the woman went away. But, says McElroy, "that's the kind of thing he has to deal with now. There was nothing he could have done to stop it. It all happened so fast."

CHAPTER

11

I AM IN HELL

"Any fool can steer a ship, sir. It's knowing where to take it."
Seaman Jamie Valentine in *The Bounty*

The Bounty was promising. With a script written by Academy Award-winner Robert Bolt who had scripted *Lawrence of Arabia* and *Dr. Zhivago,* and with innovative New Zealand director Roger Donaldson at the helm, it had an auspicious beginning. Its $20 million budget was adequate for an epic — with no expense spared on authentic necessities, like a $4 million replica of the original ship. The story is a true one, surrendered over years to legend.

It also had a superb cast, led by the exceptional Welsh actor Anthony Hopkins as Captain Bligh and including Laurence Olivier as well as other veteran British actors in smaller roles. And it had, as Fletcher Christian, the most sought-after new young male star the industry had seen in over twenty years.

The part of the young officer mutineer had been portrayed by Errol Flynn in 1930, Clark Gable in 1935 and Marlon Brando in the 1962 remake. This time, Christian was to have been played by American actor Christopher Reeve, who had withdrawn.

The film opens with Captain William Bligh arriving by carriage for his court martial in London. He waits, resplendent in his Royal Navy uniform, in the grand hall of the Admiralty, impatient, proud and silent.

The thin, reedily aristocratic voice of the Lord High Admiral intones, "The court is assembled by the Right Honorable Lords Commissioners of the Admiralty, and I quote, "to enquire into the cause and circumstances of the seizure of His Majesty's armed vessel, the *Bounty,* commanded by William Bligh, and to try the said William Bligh for his conduct on that occasion.' Surrender your sword and be seated."

The voice belongs to the venerable Lawrence Olivier, who attacks his cameo role with great panache and a startling humour. In his powdered wig and regalia, he is the very picture of late Georgian military magnificence. His presence is made awesome by the papery whiteness of his skin, his watery eyes and delicate, rather quiet delivery.

Captain Bligh is being tried a year after his ship has been seized by a group of mutineers. Bligh and those who chose to remain loyal to him were cast off the ship in a small boat and essentially left to die.

The court-martial frames the action of the film, which occurs in flashback. As the story unfolds, we witness the slow poisoning of Bligh's friendship with his deputy Fletcher Christian along with the weakening of his command. It's never a black-and-white conflict; there are mitigating, confusing elements surrounding each progressively disturbing event. Eventually the pressure builds to an unbearable level (unbearable for Christian, not for the stronger, more resilient Bligh) and their ordered world is shattered.

But at first, all is bright, good humoured and positive. Bligh comes to meet with Christian at a club, where his dissipated fellow gentlemen of the Royal Navy have been drunkenly engaged in placing bets on the probable death of an unconscious companion. Bligh asks his friend to sign on for a long scientific based trip on a ship he's captaining, to which Fletcher immediately agrees with pleasure. Bligh then ceremoniously displays a coloured drawing of a breadfruit plant. Christian is puzzled and amused. When Bligh explains that he's been commissioned to take breadfruit plants from Tahiti to Jamaica to provide "cheap fodder for the slaves on the plantations there," Christian shakes his head and chuckles, "It lacks glory, William." Bligh, a trifle testily, answers, "I don't have your connections, you see, Fletcher. I want to make a name for myself before I'm too old." Fletcher, still puzzled, retorts, "And this green-grocery trip'll make your name?" In response, Bligh eagerly unrolls a chart, showing his friend the route he's planned. His objective is to sail to Jamaica around Cape Horn, circumnavigating the world. It will be a late blooming and the making of his career.

In this first exchange, we see the warmly affectionate relationship between Fletcher Christian and William Bligh. It's obviously laced with mutual respect and a common view of the world. We can imagine their having shared seagoing adventures together happily as commander and deputy. At Bligh's dinner table we can tell that Christian is a frequent guest; he's like an uncle to the Bligh children.

But real clues to Christian's character are few. We get a vague idea that he's wealthier than Bligh, and comes from a better family (officers were often third sons of aristocratic blood), but we know nothing more about his background history.

Would another actor have imbued Fletcher Christian with idiosyncrasies such as snobbishness, selfishness or narcissism? Might he have been spoiled, easily led or romantic? Someone so *simpatico* with Bligh most probably would not possess these traits in an obvious way. But an audience would need to see them surface from the beginning. Without help from the script to make that happen, the actor playing Fletcher Christian is trapped within the parameters of whatever behaviour he's called upon to deliver. He can't simply make up character traits the script doesn't provide.

One of Mel Gibson's assets as an actor is his simplicity. It's a rare commodity in a performer and in conjunction with a fully realized character it is very pleasurable to watch. But a character that is limited on paper demands a more flamboyant, explorative approach. The actor almost has to become a writer as he's acting, to second-guess the hidden meaning behind character, relationships and plot. It's not something everyone can or should even be capable of — especially simple actors like Mel Gibson.

He knew there was a problem: "When I got the script, I thought, 'What am I going to do here?' The character was lacking, and the only place to do something was in the mutiny scene when he flips out."

And here was where Gibson took a big risk. The morning they were to shoot it, he rethought and virtually rewrote the scene, deciding that Christian would have to have become so unhinged that his only recourse was to threaten to kill Bligh and then himself. As the cameras rolled, he completely let go emotionally and unleashed a frighteningly visceral diatribe, more of a long, articulated primal scream than a speech. It surprised everyone, including Anthony Hopkins, who nevertheless enjoyed its spontaneity and responded in kind. When Donaldson yelled "cut!" the crew burst into applause — a very rare occurrence in filmmaking.

Whether Mel Gibson's interpretation of the scene works or not is left to the viewer to decide. It's certainly the moment everyone remembers when talking about the film, but it wasn't particularly well received by the critics. Again, the underpinnings of the screenplay seem to be at fault. Andrew Sarris, in *The Village Voice,* put it this way: "Poor Mel Gibson never got much more than stage directions, thereby making his crack-up scenes seem more hysterically inexplicable than they have any right to be." Almost every review mentioned the problem. In *The New Yorker,* Pauline Kael wrote, "There doesn't seem to be any character written into the role of Christian . . . in his emotional outburst during the mutiny he seems to be having a nervous breakdown."

That's probably fairly close to what Mel Gibson intended. His roar "I am in hell!" was so transparently borne of truly felt frustration that, when you watch it you just can't doubt its genuineness. If it was inappropriate, as some reviers suggest, that is once again, the fault of the script for not giving the scene any substance in the first place.

When he was faced with a clearly defined objective, however, the film worked. The love scenes with Christian's Tahitian princess Mauatua, played by Tevaite Vernette, are sincere and effective, and "his eye contact with her is the stuff of which a new sex symbol is made," according to one reviewer. Throughout the film Mel Gibson is committed to the role despite its limitations and he performs it as well as he can. That makes the difference between what might have been a complete disaster and an entertaining film experience, which is how it turned out.

There are many notable elements in the film, among them the breathtaking storm sequence as the *Bounty* attempts to round Cape Horn. Anthony Hopkins' repressed and agonized Bligh, who may even be suffering from latent homosexual yearnings, is constantly interesting. There are solid performances from everyone, including Daniel Day Lewis as a resentful officer and Liam Neeson as a troublemaking seaman.

Critically and financially the film was disappointing. The gross in the U.S. was only $8.6 million, which for a $20 million epic picture was abysmal. By and large, the critics blamed the script and praised director Donaldson, the film's performances and the lush cinematography by Arthur Ibbetson. Their assessment of Mel Gibson's performance was nearly unanimous. It was summed up intelligently by *The Wall Street Journal,* which said, "His character is too sketchy to be complex and too wishy-washy to be an uncomplicated but convincing hero. This is disappointing because when you put Mr. Gibson in front of a camera, heat does emerge; he crackles on screen with a presence that goes beyond good looks or acting ability. But even a hot actor like Mr. Gibson can't raise this Mr. Christian's appeal higher than lukewarm."

The Bounty, which Mel had begun immediately after *The Year of Living Dangerously,* was to be followed that same year by three other ambitious films. Each time, as the rising star to whom many people's artistic and financial hopes were tied, Mel Gibson would put everything he had into the job.

It's something for which he's developed a reputation over the years. Jeffrey Boam, the *Lethal Weapon* screenwriter who's worked with Mel Gibson many times, elaborates: "He always plays with complete conviction. He uses every resource at his command, and he never coasts through a performance. He takes every role so seriously. Mel *always* gives a hundred percent."

That year, the year of *The Bounty* and then *The River, Mrs. Soffel* and *Mad Max Beyond The Thunderdome,* would be a true test. It was demanding, backbreaking work. Film acting is difficult; each day brings a new mental and physical challenge, a new reason to doubt your abilities, lose your courage, want to give up and go home and hide. In film, unlike theatre, once the day is over, you don't get a second chance; you can't go back on stage in front of a new audience the next night or in three weeks and try something new. When it's on celluloid it stays there. So each day of shooting a film is a mine field, especially when you care a great deal and you're doing everything you can to make it right.

Mel Gibson, still in his mid-twenties, had been handed a gigantic responsibility. Not only did he need to fulfill the creative requirements of leading roles in some of the most significant Hollywood pictures of the year, but he also had to answer to the entertainment press, many members of which found in him the most exciting new personality they'd seen in decades.

There are some people in show business who are drawn to notoriety like moths to a flame. Their whole reason for being a performer is to become *famous*. They live in the spotlight, and they love it. Then there are others for whom fame is a side effect, even something to be suffered.

Say you like yourself and you're happy with your family and you like what you do and happen to do it well. Maybe that's all you need. Maybe you don't need hype or a spread in *People* magazine. In fact, maybe it all makes you a little sick. When you're suddenly standing at the top and you're not *quite* ready to be there, what do you do?

CHAPTER

12

THE FORCES OF NATURE

"I dreamt about the river last night. Only it wasn't the river; it was a big snake. I couldn't find the head of the tail of it. And it had me wrapped up so tight I couldn't breathe."

Mel Gibson as Tom Garvey in *The River*

Tom Garvey was a role Mel Gibson coveted. He liked the man's reticence and simplicity. He identified with his devotion to his family and his rural work ethic. He appreciated Tom Garvey's individualism — his stubborn, undeviating focus on doing, against all odds, what he knew was the right thing.

Sometimes an actor's feeling for a role is instinctive, from the moment he sees the first page of the script. When that happens, the actor's affinity for the character is like love at first sight. It feels as if he's born to play the part. He can't imagine anybody else doing it. When Mel Gibson read *The River,* he wanted to play Tom Garvey.

Mark Rydell, who'd made the widely-praised 1981 film *On Golden Pond,* was directing this new picture, which would star Academy Award-winner Sissy Spacek as the wife of a Tennessee farmer whose home and family were threatened by both human and natural forces.

It was the year of the "country" movie. In 1984 three films about rural America, *Places of the Heart, Country,* and *The River,* would be released. All three dealt with the struggle of the American farmer to survive in the face of recession, official indifference, natural disaster and capitalistic greed. During the 1980s, when urban standards of living were spiralling upwards and the economy had hit a new high, the farmers of the nation were suffering. An American tradition — that of the small farm — was in trouble, and there was a confusion of possible causes, from the government policy of David Stockman to local mismanagement and opportunism. The real, underlying reasons for the decline of the American farm are extremely complicated. Farm subsidy programmes, foreign grain deals and crop surplus contracts have changed what was originally a simple and straightforward way of making a living into a risky and often unfulfilling endeavour.

The American farmer is caught in the middle of this confusion, trying to adhere to the values handed down by generations of hard working country people, while struggling to wade through an increasingly deep financial morass. This is the image that Hollywood brought to the screen in 1984, and whether or not it was accurate, it provided filmmakers and their audiences with an emotional frame of reference. The American farm has been thought of romantically, in Hollywood at least, since Henry Fonda gave his heartrending "I'll be there" speech in *The Grapes of Wrath* and Judy Garland came back to the farm from the land of Oz. In 1984, it was time to romanticize them again.

When Mark Rydell was told that he should consider Mel Gibson for the part of Tom Garvey, he had mixed feelings. Although he'd admired Gibson's work in previous films and greatly respected his acting abilities, he'd been set on using an American actor. He was concerned about trying to overcome what seemed to him to be deeply ingrained Australian mannerisms and a strong accent. "I'm an ex-musician," he said at the time, "and I'm very particular about accents."

He met Mel Gibson once, just before the actor was due in England to begin work on *The Bounty*. Mel understood his concerns, but was so intent on playing the role that he wouldn't take no for an answer. He begged him not to cast the part until he returned from England, and Rydell agreed.

In London, Mel found an excellent dialect coach named Julie Adams. He worked with her assiduously, between rehearsals and studio filming on *The Bounty,* to consider Mel Gibson for the part of Tom Garvey, he had mixed feelings. Although he'd admired Gibson's work in previous films and greatly respected his acting abilities, he'd been set on using an American actor. He was concerned about trying to overcome what seemed to him to be deeply ingrained Australian mannerisms and a strong accent. "I'm an ex-musician," he said at the time, "and I'm very particular about accents."

He met Mel Gibson once, just before the actor was due in England to begin work on *The Bounty*. Mel understood his concerns, but was so intent on playing the role that he wouldn't take no for an answer. He begged him not to cast the part until he returned from England, and Rydell agreed.

In London, Mel found an excellent dialect coach named Julie Adams. He worked with her assiduously, between rehearsals and studio filming on *The Bounty*, to develop an authentic Tennessee accent. Finally, it was time to go back to Los Angeles for a second meeting with Rydell.

"He came back," recalls Mark Rydell, "and he came to my house and started reading the script, talking, reading the newspaper — in this perfect Tennessee accent. I was really impressed, even when he stood next to Sissy, who's like a tuning fork when it comes to accents. He had damn well done it."

Mel Gibson, characteristically, plays down the excitement he felt when he won the role. "I was one of the guys Mark Rydell looked at," he says. "We had a yap and I went away. I came back, we had another yap, and I was on."

Shooting was to be on location in eastern Tennessee. Producers Edward Lewis and Robert Cortes had spent hours in helicopters surveying possible sites in Kentucky, Ohio, Pennsylvania, North Carolina, South Carolina and Illinois. They settled on a section of rolling countryside surrounding the Holston River northeast of Knoxville. Universal Pictures purchased 440 acres along the river and turned it into a farm.

There was no artifice here. The fields were ploughed and real crops were planted. Real farmhouses and barns were built, along with chicken coops, corrals and pigsties. The Garvey farm was created with weathered wood to duplicate the aged homesteads that proliferated along the Holston River Valley.

Then the production crew worked with the Tennessee Valley Authority and U.S. Army engineers to build a temporary dam that would enable them to create the flood sequences. The goal was to establish a real environment for the Garvey family to live in. Every detail was attended to, down to stains around the doors and windows and foot paths worn between the farm buildings.

The actors were brought to the location a month ahead of time to enable them to get used to their new home. Mel Gibson learned to drive a tractor and handle farm equipment from neighbourhood farmers while Sissy Spacek spent a lot of time in the kitchen, baking bread and pies under the supervision of various local women. "By the end," she says, "I had people standing in line for my pies."

All of this preparation gave the actors a solid groundwork, a comfortable level of reality on which to create their emotional world. Mel Gibson's body curved into the seat of the corn picker as if he'd been riding it all his life; Sissy Spacek's hand shot out to jiggle the stuck drawer where the measuring spoons were kept as if it were second nature, which, by that time, it was.

It was a grown up, expensive game of Let's Pretend, and a lot of Universal's money was banked on it.

The film begins with a breathtakingly photographed sequence, accompanied by John Williams' tender, flute-dominated music, of the swollen river and its lushly verdant banks, on the rocks of which stands a young boy, fishing in the mist. Thunder rolls in the distance and the boy looks up. We read on his face that it's a familiar and not necessarily welcome, sound. Raindrops start to fall. They hit leaves and plop onto grassy banks already green with moisture. The boy gathers his fish and hurries toward home, reaching the comfort of his farmhouse kitchen as the torrent begins. Sheets of rain fall relentlessly on chicken coop, empty tractor and tin barn roof. The farmyard puddles widen and its surface turns to mud.

Now begins a harrowing flood sequence (the film's first of two), in which the family of four desperately attempt to save their livestock, their personal possessions and their own lives. Tom Garvey, in trying to hold back the water's inexorable attack on his land, overturns and is pinned under his bulldozer, while his wife and eleven-year-old son struggle to set him free in the rising flood. The smaller Garvey child, a six or seven-year-old girl, watches, transfixed with terror, her face pressed against the window of their pick-up truck, repeating the mantra "Daddy, Daddy, Daddy" as if it will save her father from his imminent death.

This is our introduction to the Garvey family, and it's enough to make us care about them for the duration of the film, whatever other limitations get in the way. The story of *The River* is a melodrama, but that's not to say that because of that it's inferior. Melodrama is as American as apple pie, and we understand it in the same way. It's as bitter-sweet, syrupy and easily swallowed, if you're in the mood.

Sissy Spacek was nominated for another Academy Award for her work in this film. She plays Mae Garvey with a spirit and warmth that defines the movie, and makes everything else seem to fall into place. Her relationship with Mel Gibson as Tom Garvey helps us to comprehend and embrace the world we're watching.

There's also an especially strong supporting cast. Scott Glenn gives the part of the villain and Tom's rival an intelligent, complex subtlety. The two children are both beautifully played in low-key, natural performances by Shane Bailey as Lewis and Becky Jo Lynch as Beth.

Mel Gibson is likeable, open and completely sincere as Tom. His character is essentially uncommunicative, and so it's up to the camera, the story and his face to inform us about Tom's inner feelings. But we see them clearly, and that's because Mel Gibson feels them clearly. He doesn's need to *show* them to us; he needs only to feel them. In his days at the National Institute, one of his teachers had said that "everything that was happening inside him could be seen on his face." Nearly ten years later, the part of Tom Garvey was a true test of that facility.

Having been converted, Mark Rydell was Mel's most vigorous champion. "I've never been so enthusiastic about a leading man," he declared. "He has the roughness of McQueen, the gentleness of Montgomery Clift, the sexuality and charm of Gable." As they were shooting the film, Rydell also grew to respect Mel's way of working.

'There's no conflict in him about commitment; he has a kind of relaxed maturity.''

Sissy Spacek found him intensely committed, as well. ''He was really plugged into the role,'' she says simply. ''He's a great actor.''

As shooting progressed, Rydell marvelled during the rushes (daily screenings of the rough, unedited results of the previous day's work), at Mel's power under the talented eye of the cinematographer Vilmos Zsigmond. ''I don't think it's just physical beauty,'' he said. ''There are many men like that who haven't become superstars. He has a kind of electrical intensity that's somehow controlled.'' And then there was his undeniable sexuality. ''Women moaned during his closeups,'' says Rydell. ''It was audible — and justified. He has a really intense heterosexuality that we haven't seen in the movies for a long time. He's very clearly male and at the same time very sensitive, very affectionate, very respectful of women.''

Things looked good. With two magnetic, accomplished actors and an equally adept supporting cast, a magnificently authentic setting, a sensitive and communicative director, a lovely score, a director of photography who has been labelled a ''genius'' and a compelling, emotionally-charged theme, it should have been the blockbuster hit that everyone expected.

But something went wrong with *The River* and it's hard to pinpoint what. The reviews are so caught up with the other ''country'' movies of the time that they don't seem to be analyzing this film on its own merits. Most critics seemed to be upset at the fact that the story was so full of symbolism (a trapped deer in the middle of an iron foundry, a woman spitting at Tom Garvey in a Christ-like procession through a gauntlet of striking workers) and so simplistic. Gaylyn Studlar writes in *Magill's 1985 Cinema Annual* that, "*The River* reduces everything to morality defined in black-and-white terms."

This assessment may apply, but it doesn't have to be a pejorative; it's not necessarily the basic reason for the film's artistic weaknesses. Many movies over the years have dealt with morality that way; scores of good films are underpinned by simple conflicts between good and evil. Perhaps it's bothersome in *The River* because it's too clear-cut, too predictable, especially at the end. When Scott Glenn's character, Joe Wade, arrives at the Garvey farm with an army of men he has paid to destroy their dam the crisis feels manufactured, like one too many pieces of the narrative puzzle are falling neatly into place. The assembled crowd, influenced by Tom Garvey's obstinate idealism, turns against Joe Wade and helps the Garveys. At this point the symbolism (their rolling Joe Wade's jeep into the gap to stop the flow of water), is unsubtle.

It also seems as if there is just *too* much disaster, as if this film is too much like *The Poseidon Adventure* to be a truly sensitive movie. The camera work is so spectacular, the acting so powerful and the setting so impressive that it's difficult to come to such a disappointing conclusion about the story itself, but it's eventually inevitable. The screenplay, by Robert Dillon and Julian Barry, is fine in its message, dialogue and transitions; it's the story line — the plot — that falls short.

Not every critic was cynical about *The River,* however. Rex Reed raved that the film was "a shattering emotional experience, a film of inspiration and dreams that embraces the most durable human values . . . a great film, full of passion and decency, about real people whose patriotism is all but extinct. In a time of smashed hopes and trashed values, *The River* is something of a blessing." He called Sissy Spacek "breathtakingly vital and alive" and Mel Gibson "vulnerable, strong, full of integrity and charisma."

Possibly because of the other similarly-oriented films released that year, or perhaps because he was still fighting the image of *Mad Max,* Mel Gibson was treated by most critics, however, with a peculiar blend of vitriol and bored dismissal. Some reviewers seemed even to have something personally against him. In viewing the film now, one can't help but enjoy his canny and skillful grasp of the character, his emotionally accurate transformation into Tom Garvey. He made the part completely his and gave it substance.

But you'd never know it from the reviews. *The Village Voice* was particularly nasty, about the film as a whole as well as Gibson's performance in it. "On Swollen Pond," ran the headline and it got worse. "This couple comes dangerously close to being Donny and Marie on the prairie," it hoots. And "I kept waiting for someone to suggest to Gibson, who has never looked prettier, that he could buy back his mortgage in a month if he went into modeling." Why was everyone so angry?

That review gives us a big hint. Being good looking, when you are a serious actor, isn't necessarily an asset. It takes a lot more wisdom, determination and persistence to make somebody (or an audience), take you seriously if you've got a pretty face, and that's especially true for a man. Look craggy, lopsided or have an otherwise not-so-beautiful countenance and its' owner has already won half the credibility battle. You think to yourself, "Why would an ugly guy like that be an actor if he weren't brilliant?'' Conversely, when you gaze at a gorgeous face you tend to think, "This guy obviously got into the business on looks alone. He *can't* be any good."

Today Mel Gibson, at the age of 36, has a couple of lines on his face, and he's being taken more seriously. Is it accident? An informal poll taken in Hollywood recently revealed that, in the industry at least, most people think Mel Gibson was vastly underrated in his earlier film work. They point to the relaxation and ease with which he accomplished roles like those of Tom Garvey, Guy Hamilton and Frank Dunne. They mention his unerring honesty, his unique style, his uncanny ability to mesmerize an audience.

The River grossed a disappointing $8.8 million in the United States. Its "negative cost" (that is, what the film cost to produce before marketing and prints), had been an estimated $21 million. It's been moderately popular as a video rental film, but will never be considered a commercial success.

By the time the film was released and Mel Gibson received his critical pummeling, he had already been at work on the next endeavour, a new film directed by his fellow Australian, the highly regarded Gillian Armstrong. Life goes on.

CHAPTER
13
BETTER TO HAVE LOVED

"You mean God makes you miserable in this life so he can make you happy in the next, is that it?"

Mel Gibson as Ed Biddle in *Mrs Soffel*.

An improbable story, to be sure. True ones often are, and they don't always have neat, tidy — or happy — endings. Such was the case with *Mrs Soffel,* a film based on events that occurred in the smoke-darkened city of Pittsburgh in 1902.

Two brothers, Ed and Jack Biddle, were sentenced to death for the murder of a grocery store clerk. They were known robbers, but their conviction for murder was widely considered to be a miscarriage of justice. This belief was a popular one, especially among the women of the city, because the Biddles happened to be winningly handsome young men, and they made very romantic tragic figures.

As the story goes, the wife of the prison governor, in attempting to lead to Biddles toward religion, fell in love with the older brother, Ed and engineered their escape the night before they were to be executed. At the last moment he begged her to accompany them. In her nightgown, she left her husband and four children to be with her lover, knowing she was giving up her whole existence to do so. It caused a sensation, with atmosphere, characters and a plot that were worthy of a Theodore Dreiser novel.

The movie is unusual, dark (physically and spiritually) and well crafted by its director, Gillian Armstrong. She was the first and so far is the only woman to have directed Mel Gibson on film. Their collaboration, along with the performance of Diane Keaton in the title role, that of the gifted Matthew Modine as Jack Biddle and the support of a superb cast, resulted in an artistically distinguished and critically acclaimed piece of work.

"*Mrs Soffel* stands as one of the best American films of 1984, offering near-peak work from all concerned," said

The Los Angeles Times. "Mel Gibson shows more range than he ever has," said *Newsweek,* "he makes his sharpest impression here." *The New York Times* praised his "genuinely solid performance" and called him "virility incarnate."

The first half of the film is bleak and so dark it's sometimes difficult to follow the action. Diane Keaton as Kate Soffel is a sickly neurotic who wakes screaming with nightmares. She is caught in her own mental darkness, trapped in a sad, lonely marriage to a man she no longer loves. She exists for her children, and here Keaton brings a delightfully poignant sense of fun to her role, a joy that seems all the more precious when we watch it crushed by her dour husband who is played with his usual aplomb by Edward Herrmann.

Kate Soffel has made it her business to deliver Bibles, blankets and words of comfort to the inmates of Allegheny County Prison where the Soffel family has adjacent living quarters. Kate is a zealous, well-spoken proponent of the Christian message and wins first the guarded respect and then the love of condemned Ed Biddle.

When they first meet, Ed has attacked a guard and is running from his cell. He charges blindly into Kate Soffel, knocking her down and impeding his own escape. He is beaten by the guard and shoved back into his cell, bleeding. Mrs Soffel, instead of retreating in fear, hands him her handkerchief through the bars, imploring him to wipe the blood from his face.

She asks him if he would like a Bible. He flashes her a charming grin and answers, "No thank you, ma'am. We're gonna die, but we're not *that* desperate."

As he's being led to solitary confinement, he cries

earnestly over his shoulder, "Mrs Soffel! What kind of flower would you say that is, right there?" holding up the corner of her handkerchief. "I don't know," she responds, taken by surprise. He presses on, "Would you say that that's a violet? I think it's a violet, don't you?" She pauses for a long moment, and finally answers, "Yes." As he's being pushed roughly through the iron door, he shouts back, "I think so, too."

Later, she's standing before his cell, and he reads her a poem he's written:

Just a little violet, from across the way
came to cheer a prisoner in his cell one day.
Just a little flower, sent by loving hand
has a kindly meaning that true hearts understand.
Just a little violet, plucked with tender care
God has smiled upon it and its sender, fair.
And soon that little token, wrapped in hands to neat,
rests quietly within a grave in which a heart that's true has beat.

She's touched to the quick. She asks why he has written the poem for her, and he replies, fast as lightening, "What makes you think I wrote it for you?" It makes her smile, he grins back, and their love affair begins.

The connection between Diane Keaton and Mel Gibson is lovely to watch, not only because there's sexual tension but also because two good actors are really bouncing responses off each other. They are definitely in the same centre court, hitting the tennis ball back and forth like Jimmy Connors and Bjorn Borg on a good day. Mel Gibson is every inch the irresistible charmer, overwhelming her with his disarming, almost childlike candour. This ingenuousness, combined with his undeniable masculine presence and his pure physical beauty, make the idea of any woman's leaving her husband and children to be with him absolutely believable.

There's more to him than that, however. He grows dependent on her, and is not afraid to show it. So we are given Ed Biddle the character as a complete, well rounded person, with a real vulnerability. This element shows up especially clearly in the bedroom scene toward the end, when Ed and Kate are as close as two humans can be, face to face, eyes to eyes on the pillow, making sombre, awful promises to each other. He buries his head and then his body in her, trying to sink into her very being for comfort.

The three fugitives are heading for Canada in a sleigh pulled by two tiring horses. They are overtaken by a large posse of men who surround them. As she realizes there is not longer hope, Kate begs Ed to keep his promise not to allow her to be taken alive. She implores him to kill her, and, as they pledge their love again and again, their faces touching in agony, he pulls the trigger. Ed and Jack Biddle are subsequently gunned down in the snow, crawling desperately away from the army of men on their trail.

It's an American tragedy and its appeal comes from its devotion to reality and the feeling of the period. Russell Boyd's camera work is exquisite, seeming, as one critic put it, to be "inspired as much by Alfred Steiglitz photographs and Edvard Munch paintings as by the realities of industrial pollution in 1902 Pittsburgh." Another reviewer called the visual images of the film "muffled, claustrophobic beauty" and says the outdoor sequences have "the look of a rural idyll painted on old porcelain."

Gillian Armstrong, with only two previous films to her credit, both of which had garnered high praise, was showered with further kudos. "The film affirms Armstrong's arrival as a director of the first rank," said one publication. And Gillian Armstrong was pleased with Mel Gibson's performance. "Mel has a very special quality," she explains. "He can be both dangerous and romantic at the same time, and that's rare." She spoke warmly about his working relationship with Diane Keaton. "She would watch Mel during rushes and be in tears."

On his part, Mel was matter-of-fact about the character: "He's a man who is following his own passions. He hasn't had much moral guidance of any kind. Yet to himself, he's a moral man."

Mel had like the script from the first time he picked it up to read it. "I look for a script that I can read in one sitting," he says. "The minute I put it down, there's a reason to put it down. They're never perfect, but you can always get excited by one for different reasons."

"What appealed to me was the bars," he goes on. "It's a major dramatic device. You have a man and a woman and the way they relate, and you have an obstacle — the prison bars. It's interesting how they work to get around them, and eventually they lose them. There's always a good obstacle in a good love story."

Notwithstanding its strong woman's message, its dramatic conceits and its plot twists, *Mrs Soffel* is, indeed, "a love story, above and beyond everything else," as Gillian Armstrong attests. "That old saying — 'it's better to have loved and lost than never to have loved at all' — that's the theme of *Mrs Soffel.*

And Mel Gibson knows how to touch the real core of a character in love. One of his gifts is his ability to care so deeply as a character that you simply have to care with him; you recognize what he's feeling, you remember being in love like that, you identify. Writer Stephen Schiff says, "His best performances are in romantic roles, like the ones in *Tequila Sunrise, Mrs Soffel* and *The Year of Living Dangerously,* roles in which his boyish gusto can come to seem something more: ardent, overwhelming sensual."

He also seems to fit perfectly into the look and feeling of the turn of the century, with its innocence and moral simplicity. That essential element in a good actor's performance, "actor's faith", was at work in full force in *Mrs Soffel,* throughout the cast. It's doubly important in a period story, because sinking into another time, with its differences in language, mores, attitudes and social conventions, can come almost instinctively if there's enough faith, enough belief in the imaginary reality. When it works, the experience is strangely supernatural; you find yourself responding spontaneously in a way you'd never have thought you could. Logically, you and the actors know it's all coming out of the imagination, but it doesn't *feel* the way. It feels as if another person from another time, with another mind and soul, has taken over. The modern self recedes and the character takes over.

To accomplish this takes intellectual preparation, of course. Research, digging into historical detail, getting a feeling for the time, the place and the people in it. Mel Gibson, like most actors, enjoys the process and finds it absolutely necessary. "Otherwise, I don't feel safe," he admits. "I like to have a base. You can eventually just forget most of it, but the security and confidence you get from having done the research is good. But it's not fear that makes me research; it's *interesting*. You learn about a lot of things."

The artistic success of *Mrs Soffel* far surpassed its commercial impact. It was marketed modestly, at the end of the year, with a minimum of publicity. Its budget of $14 million (well spent, according to industry experts, on what was considered by most to be an elegant and cohesive example of heartfelt filmmaking), was only fractionally offset by a domestic gross of $4 million. The lack of box office excitement was blamed on a "downer" ending and a measured, intelligent approach to what might have been flashier material. *Mrs Soffel* is still an underground favourite of film buffs, however and a special gift to fans of Mel Gibson's still underrated acting style. As one reviewer put it after watching his performance in *Mrs Soffel,* "He could be in danger of becoming the movies' incredible hunk; he's a real actor, and he needs real parts like this to play."

Mrs Soffel had been physically demanding for the cast and crew; its outdoor sequences, including sleigh chases, gunfights and jumping from moving trains into the snow, had been filmed in bitterly cold weather in Canada. The achievement took its mental and physical toll on everyone concerned.

Mel Gibson was about to tackle yet another project in 1984, and this one would be even more difficult in terms of its physical requirements. George Miller was shooting *Mad Max, Beyond The Thunderdome* at great expense and in several locations throughout Australia. And there wouldn't be much time to breathe between films.

Mel Gibson was twenty-eight years old and he had become an icon. During this frenetic year of film-making, he'd also become the father of a fourth child and third son, Will. Robyn and his family were his anchor, but there had been hardly any time to spend with them. He got dozens of scripts every month from eager directors, writers and producers. His film performances were dissected, resented, adulated, attacked and adored. His public, watching him through the eyes of the press, seemed like a kind of cannibal machine ready to devour him.

Talent can be a fragile commodity, and when it belongs to someone who'd rather not talk about it, or himself, too much public exposure can be threatening. Some people thrive on that exposure; others gasp in the rarified air and long for real life again. Mel Gibson simply wants to do his job the best he can, and sometimes his popularity is tough. "There are certain expectations," he explains, "which really go against what you're trying to do, if you're trying to find your way into a role or a character who's different. It's difficult to be totally believable when there are expectations involved [for the audience], when they're not seeing you for the first time. You have to try twice as hard. Although you get the opportunities, it's harder to make them work."

Pressures were building from several directions during that landmark year of 1984, and Mel Gibson began to feel them. Like everyone, he has a dark side, a part of him that makes everything look black. But he's also an artist and he's Irish as well, which can be a volatile combination, emotionally at any rate. The attributes that make for poetic intensity and true dramatic feeling can also detonate a destructive inner explosion.

During the filming of *Mrs Soffel* Mel was drinking hard. One night he ran across a red light, hitting another car. He was arrested and fined for drunk driving. His license was suspended for three months, and the studio assigned him a "chaperone" to make sure he kept out of trouble.

"What I probably needed were some guys in white jackets," he says now. "I was going around the twist. I knew I had to channel the maniac inside me. I had to get hold of it."

But there wasn't time. He had to report to *Thunderdome,* without delay. No chance to stop and think, hold the baby, take a trip, take a breath. No chance to reassess his twenty-eight year-old life and decide what direction to take. That job would fall on the strong shoulders of his wife, soon enough.

CHAPTER
14
MAX GETS WISE

"Time counts, and keeps counting . . .finding the trick of what's been and lost ain't no easy ride, but that's our trek, we gotta travel it. And there ain't nobody knows where it's gonna lead."

Helen Buday as Savannah Nix in
Mad Max — Beyond the Thunderdome

A howling wind presages the pulsing beat of a hard-driving Tina Turner rock song. We see the familiar desert landscape from the sky, a stream of dust rising from the lonely trail across it as it's slowly traversed by a camel-pulled covered wagon.

Max is back. But in a moment, he's "relieved" of his wagon and worldly possessions by an unknowing Jedediah (the Gyro Captain), whose scavenging for stray travellers' valuables is a way of life. His bizarre plane swoops down out of the sky, he knocks Max out of his wagon and runs off with the spoils. Max is left lying in the desert, unrecognized.

He dusts himself off and we see who it is for the first time. Anybody who was watching that moment in a movie theatre when *Mad Max, Beyond The Thunderdome* had just been released and die hard *Mad Max* fans were waiting for their first glimpse of their hero, will remember the screams, the spontaneous cry of, "Max!" from the Max-crazed audience.

He's dressed as Lawrence of Arabia in negative — black turban, flowing desert garments and bare feet soon to be encased in mismatched biker boots. But he has Jesus Christ Superstar hair, long and curling around his shoulders. He's a rock star warrior now, heading toward Bartertown, a seething Babylon of activity, a mud-caked metropolis run by the voluptuous Auntie Entity, Tina Turner in chain mail.

As Max enters the walled city, the atmosphere feels like a Bertolucci epic, all biblical and teeming with motley characters, including a post-nuclear money changer selling irradiated water to unsuspecting newcomers. Luckily our Max, the survivor, has a makeshift Geiger counter with him and uses it, shaking off the illicit water vendor disdainfully. "What's a little fallout, heh? Have a nice day!" the fellow cackles, receding into the crowd.

Max is there to get his possessions back, but Bartertown has other things in store for him. He waits in line for an audience with the Collector, an imposing, Pilate-like bureaucrat, who scoffs at his request for help. In Bartertown trade is the only way to get along and he must have something to offer. When Max efficiently dispatches an approaching guard, however, the Collector takes notice of his possibilities. "You that good?" he growls, grabbing Max by the collar. Max responds articulately. "Mm-hmm." "Perhaps you *have* got something to trade, after all." says the Collector. "Twenty-four hours of your life. In return, you'll get back what was stolen." Max thinks for a split second. "Sounds like a bargain," he answers. The Collector retorts, "It's not."

Max is taken through the crowded cacophony of the bazaar to meet with Auntie Entity, who greets him with smiling but wary hospitality. He soon realizes it's a test. He's suddenly attacked from behind, but fends off his opponents with style. Now, Auntie Entity is really interested. "Congratulations," she breathes. "You're the first to survive the audition." She offers Max a deal. There's someone she wants killed, and Max seems like the man to do it. But it has to be accomplished by the rules; no outright assassination. Bartertown has its standards, after all.

The forum is Thunderdome, a geodisic auditorium where gladiator-type contests decide the fate of two contenders; the motto is "Two men enter, one man leaves." When there's a quarrel in Bartertown, the victor is the one who's left alive. No jury, no appeal, no parole.

Max is instructed to pick a fight with his designated opponent, a helmeted Goliath called 'Blaster.' Blaster is the lower half of a two-man team known as "Master Blaster," the ultimate authority in Bartertown. His upper half, a dwarf who rides on his shoulders, is "Master," the brains of the operation. They control the subterranean Underworld, where great quantities of pig dung produce the methane that fuels the city. Without this precious fuel Auntie Entity and her utopian dreams are lost. She's tired of being humiliated by the little man, who has a bad habit of calling embargoes on available fuel until she publicly acknowledges his superiority. She knows she can control him if she does away with his lower half, but it must be done properly, in the Thunderdome. She's been looking for a qualified champion and Max is elected.

Auntie Entity gives Max a look at Blaster through her special periscope. Max says, "He's big. How good is he?" The Collector answers, "He can beat most men with his breath."

In the Thunderdome, before a capacity crowd, Max and Blaster are both harnessed to double bungee cords. They're unarmed, but an array of exotic weapons is attached to the upper walls of the dome. The wryly grimacing ringmaster tells Max, "Thunderdome's simple. Get to the weapons; use 'em any way you can. I know you won't break the rules. There aren't any."

They fly at each other, springing from the cords, bouncing wildly off every surface, making sporadic and painful contact. Max is, being of normal size, wildly outclassed, but his wits save him. Knowing that Blaster has very sensitive ears, Max has a secret weapon, a dog whistle, which he uses at the last possible moment to disable Blaster and bring him to his knees. Max sends his helmet flying, and discovers in looking at his adversary's face that he's really a big child; he's a victim of Down's Syndrome. Max refuses to kill him, earning the wrath of Auntie Entity, whose plot has been thwarted. But Blaster is killed by an outraged soldier anyway and Max is sent out into the desert to die.

During this first half of the film, there's an off-the-wall humour about the dialogue that hadn't been as prevalent in *Road Warrior,* but that works well within the rock-oriented, pop culture world that George Miller and co-director George Ogilvie have created. The presence of Tina Turner defines this world almost automatically; you get the picture because her personna is so specifically delineated. It's a provocative, far-out world, like the bizarre, mutant-peopled planets in *Star Wars,* and it has a *Star Wars* wit as well, that Han Solo adolescent cleverness that wins you over even as you groan. It's outrageous and naïve at the same time, harmless fun in a classic comic book way.

The second half of the film is a different kind of story, getting closer to a blatantly Biblical theme, pulling at our heartstrings and showing us a little more about Max. He's still a reluctant hero, but he learns to care for the tribe of wild children who rescue him more than he's cared for anyone since he lost his own child. The children live in an idyllic canyon called the "Crack in the Earth" and have developed their own form of civilization, complete with designations like hunters, gatherers and "little ones." They have a religion that is an obvious but amusingly interesting slant on early Christianity, with its beliefs and litany based on random information saved from the nuclear holocaust.

Their Messiah is a character named Captain Walker, whom they believe will return one day to take them back to the nirvana he came from, "Tomorrow-morrow Land." They know about this far-away place from a toy slide-photo viewer they've long cherished as a religious relic, salvaged from the wreckage of an ancient airplane.

The children believe that Max is Captain Walker, and goad him into leading them to Bartertown. There they improbably overcome every bad guy in sight. After an obligatory *Road Warrior* style chase, with Auntie Entity and her henchmen in hot pursuit and help from the irrepressible Jedediah, they are rescued for good and taken to the promised land in Jedediah's airplane. Max is left alone once more, to wander the wilderness.

Beyond The Thunderdome was a media event. It grossed over $36 million in the United States, profitable despite its expense. Creatively, it fulfilled the expectations of George Miller and Terry Hayes; financially, it nicely met the hopes of Warner Brothers.

Reviewers raved about the Thunderdome fight sequence and the imaginative energy of the film in general. The mid-movie change to the tribe of wild children was surprising and not universally praised, but was respected as an intelligent concept. David Ansen, in *Newsweek,* said, "*Beyond The Thunderdome* isn't a seamless piece of work; it has more notions than can comfortably fit into one story, but with crazy and beautiful Mel and Tina backed up by a raging gallery of mutant humanity, only a glutton could complain he didn't get his fill."

This third time out had been a vastly different

experience for the entire *Mad Max* family. The most significant and difficult change was the absence of Byron Kennedy, Miller's long-time friend and producer. He had been killed in a helicopter crash in 1983. The film includes a simple dedication, "To Byron" before the credits at the end, after Helen Buday's beautifully delivered speech:

> Every night we does the 'tell', so that we 'member who we was and where we came from. But most of all we 'member the man that finded us, him that came the salvage, and we lights the city. Not just for him, but for all of 'em that are still out there, 'cause we knows there'll come a night when they sees the distant light, and they'll be comin' home.

Beyond The Thunderdome was a different experience for Mel Gibson, as well. He began the film physically and mentally exhausted. He did many of his own stunts (including the entire Thunderdome fight sequence) and didn't take care of himself especially well, either. He was drinking more than was good for him — sometimes four beers in the morning even before shooting started — and was not a happy camper.

To make matters worse, it was the time of the infamous *People* Magazine article, calling him the "sexiest man alive." This was already a red flag to Mel, who had spent an entire year doing his best to achieve artistic depth in his work and who felt that he deserved to expect a commensurately serious response from the press. The reality is that the press doesn't *think* of such a title as belittling, but Mel Gibson does. He thinks lots of other things are more important and to him the title "sexiest man alive" is almost an insult.

When the writers from *People* went to interview

him on location in Australia, they reported a "slumped and sullen" Mel Gibson, and spoke in their lengthy article about his truculent, injured air and his defensive attitude. They pretty much damned him with faint praise, and even recounted his verbalized opinion of the press:

> "So here is a good opportunity for some parasite to come up and throw darts in your chest. Freedom of the press," he snorts, lobbing an expressive glob of spittle into the sand.

It was a low point, made lower because the material he was working on didn't offer a lot of emotional range of spiritual satisfaction. He did his job with complete commitment but the pressure of stardom and everything he hated about it were gnawing at him. He was stuck in the middle of a steaming, stinking desert, and there was no safety valve. A *Rolling Stone* reporter was with him toward the end of filming, after a long day and lots of beer, in the middle of the night:

> He cackles maniacally, then slumps back in his chair. "I didn't realize I was so intoxicated," he says, suddenly looking very tired. "I've been out here for ten fucking weeks."

The ability that many Hollywood stars have (Ronald Reagan is a prime example), to carry on a love affair with the press is not in Mel Gibson's repertoire. He distrusts them. He doesn't *like* them at all; it's probably because he feels their vocation is essentially dishonest. He also resents their power, and like many thoroughly masculine men, he finds it more difficult to manipulate power than to antagonize it. You can tell him until you're blue in the face that it's going to backfire, but he won't listen. He wants to fight them, and so they sometimes return the favour.

The "press" is actually a collection of human beings, as difficult as it may be for some of us to realize. They have simple needs, as we all do. A primary one is to be liked. When they feel disliked (and they do, surprisingly, have feelings), they tend to respond negatively. It's human nature.

Mel Gibson looks back at that time now with a mixture of embarrassment and regret. It's not that his opinions have changed much, it's just that he can deal with things better now. "It's hard to keep your head above water when the flood tide hits," he says. At twenty-nine he was already a superstar, having spent only a few years establishing a career that any old-time veteran would envy. He had been deluged with the kind of attention he just wasn't prepared to handle. His simplicity and honesty as a performer are not manufactured; they're real. He's simple and honest in life, too, and that doesn't necessarily mix well with the hoopla of celebrity.

When *Mad Max Beyond The Thunderdome* was over, Robyn took charge. She convinced Mel to buy a cattle ranch on 800 acres of green countryside in northern Victoria, Australia, and the family retired there for an extended rest. It's a place with no pretensions, where the locals don't care about *Mad Max* or even *Hamlet*. There's no photo of Mel Gibson hanging over the cash register in the local hardware store. The Gibsons are neighbours, not aliens. They can shop, stop in for coffee, get the local gossip and be on their way. They're at home.

"I can scream and shout and wander around the back yard singing Puccini's greatest hits in my underpants if I want," Mel says. "and no one will think I'm eccentric." He uses a motorbike to ride herd on his cattle, a necessity with so much land. He is improving the bloodline of the breed with embryo transplants.

"It's amazing how good you can feel up there," he says. "There's always something that needs to be done. Life's so much fuller."

Robert Towne has been around a long time. He's considered by many to be a genius scriptwriter who has often lent his "doctoring" skills (usually uncredited), to screenplays in trouble, including *The Godfather, Marathon Man* and *Bonnie and Clyde.* He wrote the screenplays for *The Last Detail* and *Shampoo,* as well as *Chinatown* for which he won an Academy Award.

His directing credits are not as high flown, consisting only of *Personal Best,* in 1982 and then *Tequila Sunrise,* released in 1988. The latter had been a pet project for over six years, and when Warner Brothers saw the script in 1986, they responded favourably.

Except they didn't much like the idea of the hero being a cocaine dealer. They wanted Robert Towne to change the character's criminal profession, to make him a numbers runner for a dealer of marijuana instead. Towne refused. He wanted the story intact. He felt that the seriousness of the crime made the character more interesting, and that it would be more logical that he was trying to go straight.

So the project was held up, as they say, "in development." What that means is that Warner Brothers, footing the bill for the creative development of the film prior to actual production, decided to stall.

But a star put it into gear again. And that was Harrison

Ford, with whom Robert Towne had been working while tinkering with the screenplay for Ford's upcoming movie, *Frantic.* When Warner Brothers heard that Harrison Ford wanted to play McKussic (the eventual Mel Gibson character), they happily changed their tune, and development began anew. Then a second monkey wrench was thrown into the works, this time by Harrison Ford himself. He'd had second thoughts about the ramifications of playing a drug dealer and in twenty-four hours he pulled out.

The film stalled yet again. Robert Towne tried the idea of unorthodox celebrity casting, and approached Los Angeles Lakers coach Pat Riley, to see if he'd like to play Nick Frescia (the eventual Kurt Russell character). Riley was interested, but not seriously. "He said he had a day job," says Robert Towne. Still no leading man.

Towne's wife had long been a Mel Gibson fan. She urged him to see *Lethal Weapon.* But at the time Towne thought of Mel Gibson only as a very handsome lightweight, without enough real depth to carry the part of McKussic.

Finally he gave in. "So I saw *Lethal Weapon,* and I was knocked out by him. I immediately got the script to Mel, and he said yes. Warner Brothers was thrilled."

When actual filming began, Towne was thrilled, too. Mel Gibson had no qualms about McKussic's drug dealing, because as the movie begins, he's trying desperately to quit. He understood the part's panache and could make an intense commitment to the romance of it. But underlying these surface considerations was the inner reality of the role, and for Mel Gibson it came naturally. "McKussic is a character who is, I think, very pure," says Robert Towne.

"And decent. And honest. And that's Mel. He has ferocious innocence." Towne now has great respect for Gibson's power as an actor. He says simply, "Mel made the movie work."

They were not, however, without their creative differences. Robert Towne can be extremely single minded when it comes to the way a scene, or even a specific line, should be played. "Towne is a particular kind of perfectionist," says Mel Gibson. At one point, for example, during a scene between McKussic and his son, Cody (portrayed with a natural ease by young actor Gabriel Damon), Cody asks the question, "Doesn't she like you, Dad? How come she doesn't like you?" He's referring to Jo Ann, the character played by Michelle Pfeiffer. Mel answers, "Hey, I don't know what she likes and what she doesn't like." He's somewhat flustered, put off balance by the question, because his son has just managed to hit a sore spot. "I don't know if she likes a goddamn thing. You know, there are some people in life who don't like very much of anything. You know, they just have nice manners and live, you know?"

It sounds very natualistic, as if it's not really very important where you insert the "you know's", as long as you manage to put across the meaning of the line. But not to Robert Towne. He wrote the script, and as all good screenwriters would agree, every word should be delivered in the order it's been written. Many directors and actors, of course, would (and do) *disagree*, but for Robert Towne there was a designated rhythmic purpose in the way he'd composed the line, and it had to remain inviolate.

But in the heat of an emotional connection between

two actors, in this case between Mel Gibson and Gabriel Damon, interesting and wonderful things can happen. The relationship blossoms as the actors respond to each other, and often, especially in film, the actual text of a scene takes a back seat to the intensity of the performance. Film actors, even if they've been trained on the stage, are used to this phenomenon. Their job is so immediate in front of the camera, so demanding of spontaneity, that precise rendering of the lines as written sometimes seems unnecessary, if not actually counterproductive. Even if the screenwriter has planned a laugh, that's sometimes not as important as the flow of the scene and what is happening in the moment between two people.

Here lay the conflict. Towne wanted the line said exactly as written. Mel, who has what many people call a photographic memory, knew exactly what the line was, but was allowing some leeway for creative inspiration. Towne would have none of it. When they did a take and Mel said the line a little differently, Towne would cut, and demand that it be said correctly. According to Towne, this made Mel a little angry and he said, "You mean I'm going to have to say this line the same way more than once?" Of course, Mel Gibson, being nothing if not thoroughly professional, ended up doing what his director wanted and making it work.

A little later in his career, Mel Gibson would approach a role knowing he absolutely had to say every single syllable as it had been written. The role was Hamlet, and there was no question about improvisation where that text was concerned.

There's something to be said on both sides. The "necessity is the mother of invention" school of thought holds that when you have parameters to solve specific problems. The "grasp the moment while it's raw and fleeting" school puts the priority into spontaneity and more accidental impulses.

The best kind of actor, of course, can do both things. If you can be conscious of your boundaries, perhaps even revel in them, your performance can unfold within the confines of a specific framework that will inform both the character and his or her behaviour. If you can simultaneously achieve the emotional freedom to feel fully what is happening to you during every moment, your performance will truly come alive. And all that without looking as if you're "acting." Nobody ever said it was easy. Nobody very smart, anyway.

Michelle Pfeiffer, Kurt Russell and Mel Gibson make it *look* very easy, though *Tequila Sunrise* is an elegant cat and mouse game, spiced with a language that might have come straight out of a sophisticated 40s romance like *To Have and Have Not*. Michelle Pfeiffer as Jon Ann Vallenari is stunningly beautiful and strong, soft-spoken and smart. She says the best of her lines with a kind of inner glee, that lets you know that she knows that you know they're great things to have to say to somebody.

All the love scenes are affecting. Frescia's (Kurt Russell's), speech to Jo Ann in the empty restaurant is so nakedly, desperately passionate that you start rooting for him. The scene between McKussic and Jo Ann at the kitchen table is so deliciously romantic and delicately erotic that you want *him* to win her heart. And the hot tub scene between Mac and Jo Ann redefines the word steamy.

The nice part is that it's not soft porn: it's all real romance, love the way it ought to be.

The rest of the story, however, doesn't quite work. As Pauline Kael put it, "A good melodramatic structure should rhyme: we should hold our breath at the pacing as the pieces come together, and maybe smile at how neat the fit is. Here the pieces straggle, and by the end you're probably ignoring the plot points."

McKussic and Frescia have been high school buddies, and are now on opposite sides of the law, Nick Frescia being the head of the L.A. County narcotics squad. Jo Ann owns and runs a high class Italian restaurant, where Mac is one of her best customers. This leads Frescia to believe that Jo Ann is in on Mac's drug business although he eventually discovers she's not. In the meantime, he's fallen in love with her but continues to use her to try to get information about Mac.

Now a big shot Mexican drug enforcement official called Commandante Escalante played by Raul Julia appears on the scene. He's suave and intimidating, oozing with Latin charm and reeking of danger. Later, we find that he's a double agent. He's revealed as Carlos the drug overlord, the very outlaw he's ostensibly attempting to entrap — a neat plot twist. Julia plays Escalante/Carlos with great humour and style; he's a fine foil for all the romance swirling around the rest of the movie. He and Mac have a long personal history involving a heroic act of valour in prison, during which Carlos apparently saved Mac's life. On this, Mac's reluctant fidelity to Carlos, in spite of his criminal involvement, is based. Ultimately, Mac must decide who to trust, who to defend and who to kill. It's meant to be an excruciating climax of clashing loyalties, but the story has become so over-involved that you want to give up paying attention and just worry about whether Jo Ann and Mac will ever get together. Of course they do, in a gorgeous final scene where Mac comes walking through the waves from a rescue boat and Jo Ann runs into the water to embrace him, while Nick Frescia looks down from a bluff in rueful admiration, having engineered their rendezvous.

Mel Gibson's performance was unanimously praised. Pauline Kael astutely observed in her review that the part of McKussic "gives Mel Gibson a warmer character than he has played before." *Newsweek* called the relationship between Pfeiffer's Jo Ann and Gibson's Mac "advanced chemistry." Their visual contact with each other is electric, unmistakably real. Because they are both so physically beautiful, it's an achievement that the look in their eyes is even more compelling than their exquisite outward appearances. They work together so honestly and effectively that it provides a strength the entire movie can rest on.

Tequila Sunrise was, finally, a mixed bag both critically and financially. It wasn't a failure either way, but it did fall short of some expectations. As *Newsweek* put it, "Because Towne is the legendary writer of *Chinatown* and *Shampoo* there will be disappointment in some quarters that *Tequila Sunrise* lacks the resonance of these seminal movies." Many critics who derided the plot also raved about the nuances, the rhythms, the style and the emotional heat the film engendered. Financially, it grossed in the United States a respectable $39 million (against a cost of $19 million), but it wasn't the blockbuster hit the studio had envisioned. For Mel Gibson, it showcased the kind of ardent sensuality and romance he hadn't had the opportunity to reveal before. He'd come close in *The Year of Living Dangerously,* but the overlying political concerns of that film had tempered its erotic possibilities. *Mrs Soffel* veiled his sexual power behind a modest historical scrim. Finally, in the very contemporary *Tequila Sunrise,* Mel Gibson did what most women, at least, enjoyed the idea of watching him fall in love on celluloid at least.

Vincent Canby, in the *New York Times,* wrote: "While the audience looks on in increasing bewilderment, *Tequila Sunrise,* sails away on what happens to be a gigantic cocaine high." Others, including Pauline Kael in the *New Yorker,* were more in accord with the film's intentions. "You have to be able to enjoy trashy shamelessness to enjoy old Hollywood and *Tequila Sunrise.* Robert Towne, who wrote and directed, is soaked in the perfume of thirties and forties Hollywood romanticism. Chances are you'll know you're being had, but you'll love it."

Drug highs and cognizance of a trashy confidence trick, is not quite what producers would have hoped for in reviews. But then, *Tequila Sunrise* was not quite a winner.

CHAPTER
15
MAD MAX GOES LOQUACIOUS AND LETHAL

After burying himself in four films in two years ending with *Mad Max 3 — Beyond The Thunderdome* in 1985, Mel stayed on his 330-hectare Australian ranch for eighteen months, where he dried out, got over his identity crisis and so avoided Hollywood's too-much-too-fast-too-soon syndrome.

He had plenty to do on the property and enjoyed time with Robyn and the kids. Yet he wasn't idle where his career was concerned. Mel read scores of scripts, which had been mainly sent to him from Hollywood by this agent at William Morris, Ed Limato.

"It was a good, reflective period for me," Mel told a reporter. "I had a chance to clear my head after not being able to handle all the attention I was receiving. I was getting over my confusion and getting in touch with me again. I gradually learned to relax and be less concerned with, you know, the media."

Explaining his problems and fears at a press conference, Mel opened up a little more.

"When you're living your life as normal and you walk down the street and nobody notices," he said, surprising many of the hardened Sydney reporters scribbling in front of him "and then all of a sudden that [people noticing] begins to happen, it's not a natural way to exist. You are not used to it and you think it's going to be great. But it's not. And then when it happens you can go two ways.

"You can kind of try and kill it. It becomes a problem that you can try to wrestle and fight, right? Just fight it, just be ill at ease with it, and you usually end up in a lot of trouble that way. So what you've got to do is ignore it, in a way, but not be fighting it and it'll just be water off a duck's back. I think it's something that you have to get to . . . it's hard to explain."

This was the new, contrite Mel, who would try hard to live with his fame. He would try not to be rude to reporters, whom he acknowledged were a part of the process that had changed his life, mainly for the better, at least in financial terms.

Mel likened the media to cheese cake. It was something that seemed awful until you tried to enjoy it, and once you did you could become used to it.

"You're trying to have your cake, like it and eat it too," one corruscatingly witty scribe quipped.

"Yeah," Mel said, pulling a face. "Well, maybe not. But don't write that I said you were crumbs."

Some of the journalists laughed. His relatively solitary time had not diminished his quick, sometimes nervous responses.

One reporter asked him about his drinking.

"My doctor told me my liver was shot to hell," Mel said with commendable honesty. "I decided it was time to quit drinking. The first month was awful, but now I'm happy to drink just soda water."

"Are you considering any new projects?" another media man asked.

"Yeah, we are thinking of improving our irrigation," Mel replied with a straight face.

In reality he was spending a lot of time considering new film properties. Amongst the scripts he was reading was a James Bond thriller, which Mel found "kinda boring". He was astute enough to judge that Bond had had his day and it wasn't necessarily a ticket to somewhere as it had been in the sixties and seventies. Besides, with

Russia loosening up and Communism tottering all over Eastern Europe, Bond-style espionage was passé. The Cold War was ending as the fantasy world of books and films was looking for new heroes and enemies.

After a period of rest and reflection Mel was also looking for a script that was a step up and away from Mad laconic Max. He was not keen on playing another John Wayne/Clint Eastwood "looks could kill" character. He found something interesting in a story called *Leathal Weapon,* written by a twenty-four year-old newcomer, Shane Black. The Martin Riggs character seemed to take that extra step. He was troubled, dangerous, zany, enigmatic and living personally and professionally on a knife edge. Limato negotiated a million dollar plus deal and Mel flew to Hollywood to meet *Lethal Weapon*'s director, Richard Donner (the maker of *Superman* and *The Goonies),* and co-star Danny Glover, whose recent roles had included the tyrannical Mister in Steven Spielberg's, *The Color Purple,* and the murderous cop in Peter Weir's *Witness.*

At rehearsals there was an immediate special magic between Mel and Glover and they quickly became friends.

"We had real fun," Mel said, "It showed on camera straightaway. Danny's a great talent to bounce off."

Mel was fit and ready for work and jumped at the idea of attempting to understand — however superficially — what it was like to be a cop in LA — which were the roles for him and Glover. They went on patrols with the Los Angeles Sherriff's Department.

"I went away with a deepened respect for the way they work," Mel observed. "I mean, they wake every day knowing it could be their last, a luxury most of us don't want. Cops' lives are downright tough and dangerous. "Your imagination begins to work after a few nights with the patrol," Mel noted. "You begin to see everyone — even little old ladies on the street — a different way. You understand why these guys [the police] are wired up and ready for action all the time. And you begin to see why there are marriage break-ups and suicides."

Mel lifted weights to get super-fit for the role, working hard on his upper torso and biceps, and he learnt some jujitsu and karate to make his fight scenes authentic.

From his first scene, Mel revelled in the role of Martin Riggs, the over-the-top cop, and strove to bury his image as Mad Max.

"Riggs had scenes that would leave Mad Max looking on in disdain, or walking off in disgust. I mean, the guy (Riggs) cries. Max would never have done that. It wouldn't have been in keeping with the film. It just wouldn't have worked. I thought that to give a man who is in so much pain, a bit of light would be interesting."

The first twenty minutes set the pattern for *Lethal Weapon*. Mel did a nude scene, feigned madness, cried during a suicide attempt and jumped from a multi-story building. He was warming to the character of Martin Riggs, to which Mel was bringing things he had never brought to any character before. He felt the script, as it opened out, "had a lot that others lacked in the past".

He wouldn't have said it at the time, but the way he was handling the role was giving him every chance of getting into the top drawer of modern film stars. In many ways it was a "safe" box-office story. He was a good guy, along with his buddy, and together they were fighting the very nasty guys. It was a big movie cliché, with little room for reality as the usual run of heavy violence, sickening thuds, murders, car chases, vicious fights, plus a bit of 1970s tits (a topless call girl falling from a building) and bums (Mel's), for good measure. Even the race issue was politically correct with Riggs working hand in Glover with his black, nice-guy partner Roger Murtaugh.

The meagre plot was just twisted enough to be called "different" in Hollywood. The black guy is the Vietnam veteran who has fitted snugly back into Middle America after the traumas of war. He is the happy family man who has put the war behind him. Tinsel-town hackneyed productions would never have dared to do this in the past, especially as the stable black character plays opposite the white quasi-psychotic widower with a penchant for putting gun barrels into his mouth.

And the plot? Well, for that we must return to the topless girl we left hurtling from a building. She happens to be the daughter of one of Murtaugh's Vietnam War buddies, Hunsaker. It transpires that she has OD'd, so the opening has the classic drugs, sex and violence combination, which sets the tone for the rest of the film. Hunsaker (Tom Atkins), asks Murtaugh to find his daughter's slayers. Riggs and Murtaugh pair up and hunt the murderers, who are drug-trafficking, ex-Vietnam mercenaries led by General McAllister (Michell Ryan) and his particularly rotten albino sidekick, Mr Joshua, superbly played by a well-cast Gary Busey.

Mel's Riggs is first seen drinking and belching through a haze of smoke, and even his dog seems disgusted. As written, the Rigg's character would have put off many actors. But not Mel. In fact, he took the character further than the script. His push to "the edge of the envelope" was exemplified in the memorable near-suicide scene.

Riggs, still lamenting the loss of his wife in an accident, puts his police revolver in his mouth and slowly squeezes the trigger.

"We were inside a small trailer van," Richard Donner recalled. "Mel, me and the camera operator. I checked the revolver before it was handed to Mel. Even a blank could kill (and has done so recently in incidents: Bruce Lee's son was killed in 1992 during a terrible filming accident). I left the trailer and watched the scene on a video monitor outside the van. I couldn't believe what Mel was doing. It was so real I thought for a moment that he might have slipped a bullet into the gun! Mel could have done that when I wasn't looking to maybe give him extra motivation. I stood frozen as Mel began to choke on the barrel and his finger pulled the trigger . . .

The director was about the call "cut", but Mel continued. Tears of frustration and rage began to fall as he wept openly, apologizing, as Riggs, to a photo of his dead wife. Donner waited until Mel had finished before calling for a halt. Then he rushed into the van and hugged and congratulated Mel.

"Wanna try another for safety?" Mel asked.

"No, no," a relieved Donner replied quickly. "We got it. It was perfect. Perfect!"

Donner afterwards told reporters he could not have gone through the scene again. The sequence lived up to expectations when cut and slotted into the final edit and audiences fell gravely silent during its few seconds. Some even succumbed and called out for Riggs not to pull the trigger.

Just as easy to recall for every enthralled member of the audience was the so-called "three stooges" scene. Riggs has set up two vicious drug dealers. They are mesmerised as he does a "Larry, Curly and Moe" routine, rubbing his hair and pulling a crazy face, while emitting an idiotic "woo, woo, woo, woo". For a moment the dealers are off-guard and then Mel pulls a gun on them. The lightening fast contrast from Stooge to killer-cop is stunning.

There had been no mention of this zany routine in the script, but Mel had improvised, having been a Stooges fan for decades.

"I'd been doing it since I first saw them on TV as a kid," Mel told reporters, "and the moment seemed right."

To play the fool in a deadly serious moment and make the contrast work took courage and exceptional skill. The result was a sequence that might go down in cinema history. It is capped by Riggs screaming: "Shoot me, shoot me, shoot me!" to the police when one of the drug gang is holding him as a shield. Is it the ultimate bluff, or doesn't our hero care if he lives or dies? The audience is gripped. It's totally in keeping with the off-the wall guy Mel is portraying.

Another moment drew the epithet "great" in terms of sheer entertainment. The particular scene looked as if it was lifted from Dirty Harry. Riggs tries to talk down a person who is attempting suicide by jumping from a high building. Riggs tells him he doesn't really care if he commits suicide, then quickly slaps handcuffs on the man. Instead of pulling him back, Riggs jumps from the building taking the man with him.

The word "chemistry" has been over-used in

Hollywood, but this movie thrived on it. First there was the Mel-Glover double act, which worked extremely well. Then there was the Mel-Donner symbiosis, which would prove to generate one of the most successful money-spinners ever in the business.

"Mel is a very special human being," Donner said, "the most exciting thing that's come into my life as an actor and a friend."

This admiration translated to quiet guidance on the set and a free reign when Mel wanted to let loose. The result was a winner that no one could ever have predicted.

The stunts in *Lethal Weapon* are one of its great strengths. Along with the sophisticated, extended gunplay in every conceivable locale, for Mel Gibson there are the aforementioned high jump from a building, an underwater fight in a swimming pool that's complicated by a clinging plastic cover, a house exploding in his face, a fall backward through a window, another jump from a bridge onto a crowded freeway, being hit by a moving car and smashed into the windshield, then thrown off again, and the *piece-de-resistance*, a three-and-a-half minute hand-to-hand martial arts extravaganza performed under a deluge.

All of this was accomplished with the invaluable involvement of a courageous and likeable guy named Mic Rodgers who has now been Mel Gibson's stunt double for just about every movie since *Lethal Weapon*. Mic is the one who actually gets the explosion in the face, the shards of glass in the shoulder and the air whistling past his ears as he falls from hundreds of feet. Mic also helped plan each stunt, making certain that it was safe for both Mel and himself, and anybody else in the vicinity.

To prepare for the rigors of the film, Mic Rodgers and

Bobby Bass, *Letal Weapon*'s stunt co-ordinator and a former Green Beret, worked with Danny Glover and Mel Gibson for four weeks before filming began. "We put them through a regime of shooting and a tough exercise programme," says Mic. "Not only just shooting, but tactical stuff, scenarios, so they would instinctively start doing things correctly without our having to instruct them. We went through, easily a thousand round of blanks a day, every day, on a back lot at Warner Brothers. By the time we were through, either one of them could pick up a Beretta, or a machine gun or a shot gun and know exactly what to do with it, how to be safe with it, how to clear it, how to put it together — they were really into it, they looked really good, and they worked as a team." Mic Rodgers calls both Danny Glover and Mel Gibson "handy actors", which in stuntperson language means they are athletic and coordinated enough to perform well physically while acting. It's another way of saying they can talk, walk and chew gum at the same time. They're capable, the kind of actors stuntmen enjoy working with. Especially in an action picture like *Lethal Weapon,* a handy actor makes everybody's life easier.

But sometimes, a stunt is just too risky even to involve a star peripherally. When the house explodes in *Lethal Weapon,* Mic and Danny Glover's double, Joffrey Brown, are the ones walking toward it as it detonates. This was a very complex scene to shoot, as the house had been dismantled board by board and put back together packed with explosives. There could be only one take, of course, and everything had to go perfectly. Otherwise, it would have set back the schedule a couple of weeks which would have been financially disastrous.

Mic's first concern was facial protection. He asked Donner why, on a bright, sunny day in Los Angeles, Mel and Danny weren't wearing sunglasses. Donner answered that he wanted to see their eyes. When Mic said, "Yeah, I understand that Mel Gibson gets all that money for his beautiful eyes, but I'd like to keep mine," Donner immediately understood and put his two stars in sunglasses, so that their doubles could wear them, too.

Joffrey and Mic, as Danny and Mel, were to walk toward the house and, as they hit a spot marked with an X, the button to detonate the explosion would be pushed. On the first take, they were two steps away from the X when they heard "Cut!" Donner and director of photography Stephen Goldblatt were waiting for a plane to cross the sky behind the scene, because they wanted it in the shot at exactly the right moment. So the walk toward the house had to be coordinated with the approaching plane. Three more times they began their walk, only to hear "Cut!" because the plane was too small, at the wrong angle or too low. One the fifth take they kept walking and hit the X. But there was no explosion. They heard someone say, "The plane's late!" They kept walking. Two more feet and it would be too dangerous to continue; they'd be fried alive by the blast. Finally, the house exploded and they leaped backward as planned. Joffrey began slapping Mic's back as if he were on fire, which Mic thought was a very realistic touch. He then realized that he *was* on fire. The shot ended as Mic's flaming jacket was torn off. In the editing room, it was matched with a similar shot using Danny and Mel. The scene worked. And so, magnificently, did the whole film.

Lethal Weapon took an impressive US$6.8 million in

its first weekend in the U.S. and topped the box-office for two weeks pulling in $20 million — ahead of *Platoon* and *Nightmare On Elm Street III*. This took Mel out on the promotion trail around the world again, but he was marginally less irritated by facing the media circus than before.

"Everyone seems to like it," he told reporters, adding with disarming frankness, "It is so refreshing to speak to people about a movie I've done and know neither of us had to lie about it."

He was talking about takings, for he never had to lie about his own performances in any movie, particularly *Tim* and *The Year of Living Dangerously*. It was just that this time the box-office returns were going to be huge and commensurate with his performance.

At the New York screening Mel found "people laughing at the right moments and that gave me a tremendous feeling of reward."

Others with box-office influence liked it too.

"This is the film that will finally make Gibson a megastar in this country," showbusiness commentator, Rona Barrett said in one of her widely syndicated radio reports.

This comment from Rona was double-edged after his several near misses in the U.S. — *Mrs Soffel, The River, The Bounty* — and perhaps some had doubted he could successfully break the *Mad Max* mould. But he had been dealing direct with Hollywood for a mere four years and was still just thirty-one years old.

At a Manhattan Hotel press conference he was asked a question he would hear a variant of many times in the

157

next few years. How did he feel about the violence in *Lethal Weapon*?

"I don't think it's all that violent," he replied. "I get a lot of scripts for those sorts of films and I always knock them back. What attracted me about this was an action film about likeable characters."

Mel went on to say that there would always be Mad Max perceptions about him, but that this film would remove some of them.

"Besides, Mad Max's days are numbered," he added, "maybe finished. I can't really see Mad Max IV. I think it has just about run its race. Maybe they will ressurect the poor bugger in a decade or so, but who knows?"

The Riggs character, for which Mel has a long, shaggy mane, flashing eyes and a ready, if crude wit, would enhance his image as a sex symbol. Did this bother him, he was asked.

"That doesn't worry me anymore."

"Richard Gere resents audiences responding to him on that level, do you?"

"Once upon a time it did, but now I have decided that life is too short to bother with any of that."

"You have a reputation for being, well "testy" with the media," one journalist began, "Are you mellowing?"

"I've become better at diffusing these things," Mel said as he flipped open a Marlboro box. "Before, I felt there was a responsibility to be brutally honest."

He was, he explained, less inclined to commit mediacide.

"I used to be afraid of those," he said, pointing at microphones. "Now, it's not worth getting worried about. I don't let things get to me now."

How did he learn to handle things that annoyed or upset him?

Mel opened his eyes wide at the question, leant forward on his seat and dragged on the cigarette.

"Whatever is getting to you, you must make up your mind to turn them around and enjoy them. Take the scene at the end [of *Lethal Weapon*]. In it you have a fire hydrant going, and it's damned cold . . . you can see your breath . . . it was that freezing. It [that martial arts fight sequence with Gary Busey] on and off took a week to shoot. A whole week. Now we would stop and get nice and warm and have to run under that cold water again."

"You mean you had to grin and bear it?"

"Yeah, but grin and enjoy it. I mean it was unpleasant but I had someone to share it with. When we had to go in again, Gary and I would just look at each other and start laughing."

Another reporter butted in and asked if he and Busey used stunt men.

"Not in that scene. But in others we did, sure. We'd be "stoopid" not to". He grimaced. "After the week on that final one, though I wish I had. Every bone in my body ached. But it worked really well, so it was worth it." He grabbed his ribs in mock pain. "But gee, the bones still creak from it."

"Were you a movie buff as a kid?" a reporter asked, changing the direction of the conference completely.

"Nar," Mel frowned. "I didn't go much."

"What's your favourite movie?"

"*The Godfather* is one of my favourites. I also like comedies of Ernst Lubitsch and the work of William Wyler."

"And your favourite actor?"

"Cary Grant and Humphrey Bogart, I guess. I loved Cary's comedy and I'd love to play comedy myself. I think I've always unconsciously been influenced by both of them."

"Is acting easy for you?" A truly dumb question which Mel answers with grace.

"Sometimes. But sometimes it's hard. Really hard. I think it's best to be relaxed. That's my approach. Being relaxed gives you the right foundation. Of course, you gotta do all your background first."

So you're not into method acting?"

"No way."

"How did you handle the gun-in-mouth suicide scene?"

"I wasn't off flagellating myself I can tell you that."

"You didn't think of the day your dog died?"

"Nar, that's bull. The only way to get there is to be relaxed and happy. I was actually ecstatic doing it."

"So really, you don't take acting seriously?"

"Not too seriously. It's not important enough to cause pain."

Had his period at home with the family mellowed him?

"Oh yeah," he answered. "You have to stay healthy. You have to slow down for them. You can't spread yourself too thin."

Was Mel a stern father?

"I think you've got to let them know when not to pull the bull. Otherwise they'll do it the rest of their lives."

Mel was also asked about his next film.

"I don't know what it will be," he replied. "Maybe a

sequel to *Lethal Weapon,* maybe something completely different. I've done three Max films, so I've nothing against sequels. If someone comes up with a story that stands on its own, then I'd be interested for sure.''

When prompted further, he gave a hint of his readiness to take a risk, be daring in his choices.

''Basically I like to move about a lot, step up to new territory every now and then. You get sick of eating cereal for breakfast and occasionally you like bacon and eggs. So who knows what's next?''

A female reporter asked about the nude scene in *Weapon.*

''It wasn't the first time I'd bared all,'' he responded with a grin. ''I did one in *Gallipoli* as well. It was pretty much the same — shot from the back and going away from the camera.''

''Are we ever going to see you from the other angle?'' the woman persisted.

''I don't think I'm ready for full-frontal.''

''About a billion women are,'' the reporter said. Everyone at the conference, including Mel, laughed.

When the studio minders called a halt to the quizzing, Mel picked up his cigarettes, which he had been chain-smoking, and wackily kangaroo-hopped his way out of the room on an imaginary pogo-stick.

In the month of *Lethal Weapon*'s release, Mel's good humour continued as the reviews and box-office receipts flowed in. The film had impact where others in the genre, released at the time, did not. Both *Extreme Prejudice* and *Malone* disappeared as fast as they hit the circuit. But *Lethal Weapon,* in 1987, went on to gross $65 million in its first year — at the time, the eighth largest annual take in film history.

The reviews had not all been raves, but there's a species of moviegoer that exists outside the normal loop of audience-critic influence. This sort of ticket buyer will stand in line to see *Die Hard VI* no matter what the reviews are; he wants to see the action, and he knows it's going to be loud, fast and frightening. In fact, when critics decry a film for its violence, as many of them did in the case of *Lethal Weapon,* it's actually good for business.

That's not to say that all lovers of *Lethal Weapon* are mindless action freaks, however. What this movie gave its audience was a special combination of state-of-the-art action/adventure combined with truly interesting characters and a wicked wit. Much of the humour derives from the counterpoint between Martin Riggs and Danny Glover's character, Roger Murtaugh. The contrast of the stalwart, coolheaded Murtaugh, who wants very much to stay alive, against the frighteningly unbalanced, manic Riggs is naturally comical, psychological gag that works consistently throughout the film. When they begin really to care about each other, it's a truly satisfying development.

As Martin Riggs, Gibson's unpredicatability makes the character riveting, right from the beginning. Vincent Canby's review in *The New York Times* was impressed by *Lethal Weapon.* "At one point he sticks the [gun] barrel in his mouth — and the camera cuts to a close-up of his finger on the trigger. Though this is the opening scene of the movie, and reason tells one that he can't commit suicide *yet,* Mr Gibson has such intensity as an actor that it's a legitimately scary moment."

He handles the peculiar mix of character traits with confidence, clearly understanding Martin Riggs' pain along with his bright, crazed humour and his recklessness. Reviewer Janet Maslin wrote, "Mr Gibson, all flashing eyes and crazy bravado, attacks this role with great enthusiasm. Nobody else can wave a gun at a roomful of people and cry out 'Who's next?' with his particular red-hot abandon."

But he's sensitive to the dramatic requirements of the role, as well. His Martin Riggs is "a man whose wild-eyed courage is based on having witnessed so much cruelty that he no longer cares whether he lives or dies," wrote Richard Schickel in *Time*. "Gibson knows just how to temper the gaga energy of such figures with odd bursts of sweet innocence."

Critics and audiences alike responded with admiration to Mel Gibson's personal performance. It seemed to be just the right career move at just the right time, and it re-established him as a superstar, with the stature of a younger Paul Newman or Robert Redford. It had been a gamble, as all film roles are for the actors who play them. But Mel's own taste, combined with the professional acumen of his agent, Ed Limato, the creative support of an imaginative director and an excellent co-star had sealed the deal.

CHAPTER
16

RISING SUNS AND TEQUILAS

The Japanese producer had a good look at the close up of Mel Gibson on the monitor. His face was relaxed and he didn't seem intoxicated. The producer asked the director to call "cut" and approached the actor.

"We'll go one more time for luck," the producer said. "You sure you wouldn't like tea in the beer can?"

"Nar, it's okay," Mel replied, "let's do it."

"We can put Coca Cola in there . . ."

"Coke? No way. Give me the beer every time."

"If you say so, Mr Gibson."

The producer moved off the set and whispered to the director.

"How many cans is that he has had?"

"Seven."

"God, he can hold it. Best talent we've ever had."

Mel was "back on the grog" as they say down-under, after his much publicised effort to stay off it. Yet he swore that he had cut right back and as he argued to friends, why shouldn't he "make hay" like everyone else, and what he ranks high in his list of loves in life: drinking beer. Mel was paid a tidy one million dollars for a two year commercial contract that involved a few days work. Most importantly for his image, it would only ever be seen in Japan. It might not be perceived as the wisest career move for Mel to advertise a beer but his agent would have known that the commercials would not be screened outside Japan and the fees for such work were phenomenally high. Many other Hollywood superstars — Paul Newman, for example — had done comparable work. Where was the harm?

Others such as Ronald Reagan soon after the end of his Presidency, Mel was cashing in on easy money in Japan. It was a calculated move. He had been a cult figure there ever since making *Mad Max,* which had been very successful in Japan, as had *Max 2* and *Max 3.* His continued popularity there with the release of *Lethal Weapon* made him a natural for a commercial, arranged through his agent and the William Morris Commercials division, which had had nice little earning extras for many of its clients.

Mel this time didn't go straight into another movie but returned to his Australian home for some R&R, a formula he would try to maintain for the next few years. He had time to consider his next project, something which he could fit in before the *Lethal Weapon 2.*

Even during the shooting of the original *Weapon,* Richard Donner told him it was going to be a big winner.

"He didn't say how big," Mel said, "but the studio guys were already talking about a sequel."

This knowledge helped Ed Limato negotiate a doubling of Mel's contract to more than US$2 million for the sequel plus more points — an increased share of the gross. The original, according to studio sources had topped US$100 million worldwide and was heading for more than $200 million, figures which would do a lot for Mel's increasing bankability.

He was looking for something different in a script again, his agent told hopeful producers in the middle of 1987, who were bombarding him with stories. Limato acted as the sieve, knowing better than anyone where Mel's interests and strengths were.

"It would have been a disaster for him to do another grunting *Mad Max,*" he added. "On the other hand, we had to be careful not to get hooked into something similar to *Weapon* in between two movies of the same genre.

needed something daring, yes. Maybe something a little more romantic. He needed to bat off a big name female star.''

Amongst the scripts Mel was fired to read was *Tequila Sunrise*. He was intrigued. I thought, ''well, what was that?'' But I kept reading it,'' he said. ''And I thought, ''I've got to read that again. This one is interesting''. You think ''what is going on here?''. And then it just sucks you in. That's the mastery of Robert Towne's writing.''

CHAPTER
17
THE ACTING POLITICIAN

Mel placed the beers in front of the other two men, reversed his chair, sat down at the table and zipped the top off his can.

"I want to help," Mel said, his voice fatigued and throaty as he stared through the smoke haze at Robert Taylor, "I think you can win the election."

Taylor's rugged expression broke into a grin.

"Anything you can do would be great, mate."

"Give me a look at that speech again."

Taylor slid the paper over to him.

Mel lit another cigarette and examined it.

"This is OK, fine," he said, "but you gotta get their attention, know what I mean?"

Mel shifted his chair and moved the paper so that Taylor could see it, took a pen and scribbled in the margin.

"I would be more emphatic," Mel added. "Mention child abuse, drug abuse, suicide, porn, and AIDS . . . say here abortion is ah . . . you know legalized mass murder . . ."

"That's not too strong?"

"Look, you shoulda heard Reagan at election time. He would lay out the negatives in direct language . . . he'd set it all up front — then he'd say "we have to get back to traditional family values". That was the solution. You don't have to spell it out more than that. You're after the evening TV news. You've got to grab them. Once you get elected, then you can fight to do things and change things."

Taylor sipped his beer and grimaced.

"But how do I get them to listen?" Taylor asked. "My press releases never get published. The media just won't listen."

"That's where I can help," Mel said. He looked at his watch. "Let's go get some take-away for everyone."

The three men got up and left the room. But no director called "cut": this was no scene from a conspirational political film with Mel starring as a backroom strategist. Robert Taylor was not the veteran Hollywood actor, but a twenty-seven year-old Catholic truck-driver from Yarrawonga, a small Australian country town. The meeting took place in the living room of Mel's Sydney home in late 1987 during the run-up to a Federal election in Australia. The actor's involvement was the result of his years of frustration, what he saw as politicians "ruining" Australia and the country lurching away from the values he held so dearly, particularly his religious tenets. Mel's involvement with Taylor's campaign could also have been connected with his desire and need to prove himself as a true Australian. He may have felt stateless — neither Aussie, nor American nor Irish. He was and is all these things but circumstances had made him feel rootless. His children were Australian, certainly. But what was he? And like many an actor before him there may have been a scintilla of the frustrated politician coming into play.

Mel wasn't the first world famous star to gravitate to the political arena. Warren Beatty had been a Democratic Party groupie since JFK, getting seriously involved when his good friend and the party's great strategist, Pat Caddell, guided Jimmy Carter to the Oval Office. More recently there was Clint Eastwood, who became mayor of Carmel, not to mention the twentieth century's classic example, Ronald Reagan, who worked Hollywood for thirty years before becoming Governor of California and then President of the U.S.

The parallel skills between actor and politician have narrowed down the decades, especially with the advent of TV, the main tool now in getting elected. The key attributes for winning elections — delivery of political speeches, careful presentation for TV, the candidate's right "look", the simple, clear enunciation of policy, the ability to remember the right lines at the right moment in front of the cameras for sound and visual media bites — were all skills that Mel could employ easily if he put his mind to it. And if he didn't do it himself he could at least guide Taylor.

The young truckie had crude but honest views, and he felt he could represent the disaffected anti-Canberra, anti-big business, anti-big union voter-sentiment in the country, which he thought would reject the traditional big parties. These negative themes had been turned into election winners in the U.S. for Jimmy Carter in 1976 and Ronald Reagan in 1980, and Taylor thought he could attract the disgruntled, enough to get elected and at least become a parliamentary stirrer. As a self-employed, small-businessman, he was against the big, institutionalised power moguls in the country, heavy taxation, socialism and communism and what he saw as "sloppy" humanism, which led to massive, often undeserved welfare hand-outs and which weakened the self-reliance of the individual and the nation.

Taylor spoke to the media in Reagan-like platitudes about morals and family values which encompassed the Catholic Church's dictates of a generation ago, but he became more specific when discussing farmers and small business. Mel began putting his time where his mouth was, and supported Taylor's campaign to the hilt. Once the star's committment was public, the nation's media moved in voyeuristically as Mel drove Taylor's campaign truck around the electorate seeking votes.

The campaign reached a peak in Wodonga, in the backwoods, when Taylor addressed a crowd of 2000 people from the back of a truck. Next to him and getting all the attention was Mel. The star looked uncomfortable because he didn't like crowds and the media at any time. Mel was also frustrated, because although nervous, he would like to have had his say. But this was Taylor's campaign, and Mel had decided not to steal all the limelight by addressing the assembled crowd.

Mainly farmers were from the border region of Victoria and NSW, with a sprinkling of teenage Gibson fans; they cheered and clapped as Taylor delivered his speech.

"Our nation today is suffering a massive increase in child abuse, drug abuse, suicide, pornography and the AIDS thing," Taylor yelled. Mel applauded and the crowd followed.

Later, Taylor was optimistic about the meeting.

"It had a good feeling," he said and reminded reporters that his rally had been better attended than those of the big parties. "With a little luck we can give this election a real nudge."

No one was predicting a Taylor victory, but a lot of people were ringing his office offering support and saying they would vote for him.

Meanwhile, Mel continued as the campaign driver round the Kiewa Valley trying to keep the spotlight on his man, but occasionally fielding questions from voters and the media.

"Who have you voted for in the past?" one journalist asked Mel at a small crowd gathering.

"Nobody," Mel said simply. "I don't have an Aussie passport." Again his sense of statelessness might be seen to have been a motivation.

"Wouldn't it be better to be able to vote here?"

"Why? I'm not running for office. I can do more by supporting the right guy, Robert Taylor."

The journalist scribbled but when he didn't follow up with a question, Mel added:

"I might not have a vote but I do give a hoot about what's happening in this country. I'm bringing six little Australians into the world. I'm responsible for them."

"They're on Australian passports?"

"Sure, they were born here. And I can't think of anything more challenging or important than making sure we can guarantee the future for our young ones."

Mel and Taylor met at a friend's house to watch the results on Saturday night. The early results for Indi — their electorate — were encouraging, but as the night wore on Taylor's vote slipped back to nine per cent. However, even this was remarkable considering that most other independents would be lucky to score one or two per cent. The Mel factor had certainly lifted Taylor.

"I was very lucky to have Mel's help," Taylor said. "I learnt a lot from the plunge [into politics] and quite a lot of it came from watching Mel in action. It wasn't like watching him as a character in a movie. He was speaking from the heart as any Australian family man might. He wasn't acting. Anyone who came to a meeting could see that.''

Taylor, his sincerely felt views expressed and aired, had his fifteen minutes of fame next to Mel. The truckie then disappeared into obscurity once more as an office supplies salesman. By contrast, his political mentor prepared to return to Hollywood on his rise to becoming one of the most famous faces in the world.

CHAPTER
18
MORE LETHAL WEAPONS

"He's very married and I'm very married so it felt quite strange in bed with someone other than my husband."
Patsy Kensit on her sex scene with Mel

News came through from the U.S. that the receipts for the original *Lethal Weapon* had moved easily through $200 million worldwide. Mel's new contract had been renegotiated so that he would receive ten per cent of the sequel's gross. Should it make as much as his first film, Mel would earn a remarkable $22 million.

Just before he left Australia on the now familiar Quantas trek across the Pacific, family in tow, he was asked a most familiar tricky question by a TV interviewer. How did he justify action (in *Tequila Sunrise*), as a drug dealer, then a man of sustained violence (in *Lethal Weapon*), when he espoused family values and abhorred the increased violence in society?

"These sort of films are fantasy," he said dismissively, "a harmless release and pure entertainment. People like cowboys and indians, that's basically what *Lethal Weapon* is about. Look at John Wayne movies. Pay attention to the violence in them. It'll blow you away."

Did he think there should be less violence in cinema?

"There's always more violence on the screen than I think there should be," he admitted. "I was watching *Star Wars* recently. It's so violent. But hey, violence on stage and screen has been with us for a long time. Maybe if you don't have it up there it's going to come out some place else. I don't believe that films have anything to do with society becoming more violent, because society itself has been becoming more horrendous. There are barbarians out there — people who don't know the difference between right and wrong."

Mel refused to acknowledge that what he did on screen could engender, endorse or influence anything in real life, a point with which psychologists around the world might argue strongly.

Mel bought a Malibu house from actor-singer Rick Springfield for $3.5 million and put his family there for the duration of the sequel. The good guys were Mel and Glover again, but the baddies this time were not from behind the old iron curtain, or drug dealers or even the much-maligned CIA. They were South Africans. This was not exactly new but it was considered novel for Hollywood to embrace it so wholeheartedly.

The South African consular officials were portrayed as being so rotten and evil that the audience were swayed quickly into considering them as deserving of violent destruction.

Syndicated black critic, Larry Cardinal, thought the film showed the "morality of the lynch mob. It was the first time I've ever felt sorry for the South African government. I must also question the story's morality. Riggs and Murtaugh seemed far too ready to shoot first then read the dead targets their rights after the event."

Not surprisingly, the South African government took exception to the film. "It's a Hollywood trend to make South Africans the villains," its vice-consul in New York, Paul Bryant complained. "Suddenly the Russians and the Czechs and the Cubans are good guys. Hollywood was in a quandry about who they would use as a villain, until they remembered us. Who knows who it will be next?"

Vanity Fair's showbusiness writer, Stephen Schiff, interviewed Mel on the set and found him far more relaxed than did other reporters during the making of previous films. It seemed that he was beginning to have fun in movies for the first time in ages, and with good reason.

He was a *bona fide* star now, whose name on a property meant much, including money, of which he had now had buckets.

For these reasons *Vanity Fair* had sent Schiff, who regarded himself as above chatting with anybody less than established stars, to do a cover story. *VF*'s photographer, Annie Leibovitz, captured him both clowning and serious, both groomed and unkempt, often with his beloved Marlboro in his hand. In the pictures he gave the impression of a man at ease, even though his work schedule was exhausting.

"The star turned his eyes toward me," Schiff reported, "and suddenly I find myself transfixed. They are astonishing, those eyes: pale and opalescent, with vagrant beams of light glancing from the corneas." Still no doubt transfixed, Schiff then went on to speak of Mel as a real star in the style of the 1930s and 40s . . . "He's a throwback to the age of airbrushed glamour photography and high-circulation fanzines, the age when a certain value was placed on surface glitter, on the status that limos and pomp conferred . . ."

Off the set, Mel was having a good time indulging in his infamous puns, making pratfalls, wearing coffee filters like yarmulkes and bellowing renditions of "Eidelweiss".

"I generally like to horse around, you know?" Mel told Schiff. "And I figure if you have to work for a living, you might as well make fun of it. What I do certainly isn't a cure for cancer. And one of the best things about this job is you can enjoy yourself at it almost all the time."

This was a far more confident, professional Mel than the unsure Gibson, who got nasty with reporters on the set of *Mad Max III*. He was now at home with stardom, and his manner was helping in every way — including, most importantly, his performance in front of the cameras.

Richard Donner again encouraged him to improvise and Mel was busy throwing out lines in the script on the day they were to be shot, and adding his own.

"You take the situation at hand and see what you find funny and try to introduce it," Mel explained. "You make it part of the screenplay."

He had never improvised as much before and was performing so well that much of it would not end on the cutting room floor.

An example occurred in the scene where Murtaugh finds himself sitting on a booby-trapped toilet. Murtaugh can't stand up without the bomb going off. Riggs finally pulls him off the seat and they dive sideways to avoid the blast.

A cut finds them alive and lying close amongst the rubble.

"Come on, just a little kiss before they get here," Mel says.

There was method in Mel's ad-libs. He, along with Donner, the producers and the studio were keen to make the sequel at least as good as the original.

In keeping with Mel making Riggs less neurotic and more open to an on-screen affair, was the love scene with Patsy Kensit, then the wife of British keyboard player, Dan Donovan. It took two days of filming. The media were intrigued. They button-holed the unsuspecting Patsy and asked her what it had been like.

"I kept whispering in Mel's ear, 'God I miss my husband'," she told incredulous reporters.

They wanted more detail than that. After all, wasn't

he the sexiest man alive, etcetera. What was it really like?

Patsy began by admitting that it was "very weird". Then she added: "He's very married and I'm very married so it felt quite strange in bed with someone other than my husband. Before we did the scene, the closest we got to each other was playing scrabble between takes. The first word I made was "vomit" which he thought was brilliant."

"Mind you," Patsy added. "He did tell me a lot of really dirty stories."

The journalists looked up from their notepads and tape recorders.

Dirty stories? That's it?

Patsy was miffed.

I can't see what all the fuss is about," she said angrily and refused to answer any more of the trivial questions.

Lethal Weapon II continued on its winning way with more carnage than in the original. There was a death every three minutes on average, still not up there with *Attack Force Z,* which managed a killing every forty-five seconds or so.

Yet the methods in *LW 2* were getting more graphic and gruesome. One baddie had his cranium removed by a surfboard and two more were wasted by a nail gun. A heroine drowned, cops were blown up, yet more baddies were shot in the skull, not to mention those pulverized by Mel's fists.

The actor found himself defending it all yet again and told a TV interviewer after shooting, that the movie's message was fun, not destruction.

"It's a kind of Three Stooges thing," he explained a

little hopefully and repetitiously. "Now, the Stooges didn't have semi-automatic weapons, but they had carpentry saws and shoved crowbars in eyes and stuff. It's all an illusion, this violence."

Mel was defending with good lines but was getting the message. He began to feel an urgent need to make movies that got away from the rape and pillage.

CHAPTER
19
BIRD ON A LIFE LINE

Mel had met Goldie Hawn, wife of actor Kurt (dubbed by Mel, "Kurtus Interruptus"), Russell during the filming of *Tequila Sunrise* and they got on well. So well, in fact, that they discussed making a movie together. Mel wanted a vehicle that would take him from violent drama to humour to cater for his own skills, and his public image. After all, he would only be taking his clowning around on the set formally before the cameras. Mel had been told often enough by those in the industry that he should do commedy. It was about time.

It was more than time for Goldie Hawn. She had had two recent flops with *Wildcats* and *Overboard* and hadn't had a big hit since *Private Benjamin* a decade previously. Linking up with Mel, whose star was in the ascendant, would seem to be an opportunity too good to miss.

Mel, his agent and management continued to sift through scripts and ideas, which were coming in at a rapid rate. He talked a lot about an Australian comedy concerning tea bags, but that went off the boil. A producer from Downunder spoke about Mel in a feature on the comic strip hero, "The Phantom," yet it remained just that. He was offered a motor racing story called "Champions," which later became *Days of Thunder* with Tom Cruise. Robin Hood was offered and rejected, leaving Kevin Costner to star in it.

"He was getting a wider variety of proposals than any other star in Hollywood," according to a Warner Bros executive, "and he was naturally being choosy. There were more than role and money considerations. Mel had to look ahead and see where he would go for the next five to ten years, now that he had real 'big Mo' (momentum)."

He liked a script called *Bird On A Wire,* calling

it a "frothy piece of fun and action," "funny and warm".
He linked up with Hawn, taking his biggest fee yet (around
$4 million), plus points.

In the story, Hawn encounters Mel (here a former
Sixties radical), at a filling station and recognizes him as her
fiancée of fifteen years previously, who was supposedly
killed in a plane crash. The Mel character had gone
undercover after being a prosecution witness in a drugs
trial. Predictably — and predictability in this script was a
weakness — the drug dealers he helped put away are after
him. His ex-fiancée becomes entangled in the chase — in
cars, motorbikes, planes and a rollercoaster — and their
broken romance is rekindled.

"There was a lot of promise in the script," Mel said
later while reflecting on his motives for taking the film on.
"I've always been afraid to try things like that, but I
thought I'd just dive in and see what happened."

Unfortunately there was a lot of movement on the
screen, but little at the box-office. One critic put the blame
partly on Mel, implying he had been miscast in a "laconic,
George Segal-type role". Mel seemed "better at adding
laughs to tense, dramatic situations, rather than playing a
direct comedy." Mel may also have been too young for the
part and Miss Hawn a little too mature.

The actor was circumspect suggesting the failure
might not be all his fault. The script seemed hesitant,
without a powerful through theme. It bounced from one
sequence to the next as if the actors were being tipped into
one energetic scene after another. Director John Badham
(he of *Wargames, Short Circuit* and *Stake Out*) also
thought he was onto a winner, but couldn't lift it above the
ordinary.

The script called for sex scenes but Hawn objected to them strongly.

"They were hot and heavy," she said. "So I got on to Mel and said, 'have you ever seen me do a love scene? It's just not my thing'."

Mel hardly had any choice but to agree and the actors' line of argument was that it was not a movie suitable for hot love scenes.

"It's a film about love, getting people together and remembering," Hawn said. "It's innocent. It just wasn't right to see these two people go at it together. It would be a turn off."

The writer disagreed. He had put emphasis on the natural passion created by a disrupted affair — a relationship that had never actually failed or broken down. He saw great poignancy in a strong physical coming together after long, unwished-for separation. If they were attracted as they had been in the past, it would have interest, credibility and "sparkle".

However, Hawn's interpretation held sway, not just because she was still regarded as a skilled actress. She appeared on the surface to be well-cast. Even her much-publicised fear of heights seemed appropriate, because her screams and hysteria would be real.

"They forklifted me up to the rollercoaster like a jackass," Hawn told the media afterwards. "I faced every fear I've ever had in that film, especially climbing around the ledge of a twenty-storey building."

During one take, Hawn froze and began to faint. Mel grabbed her arms and hauled her to safety.

"Make no mistake," she said. "Mel saved my life."

But he couldn't save the film.

In *Lethal Weapon,* the character Hunsaker explained to Murtaugh how he got involved in the drug trade.

"I ended up working with a group called Air America. It was a CIA front. They secretly ran the entire Vietnam war out of Laos."

Hunsaker goes on to tell of his employ with Shadow Company, including a list of sources in Asia for shipments of heroin.

". . . (they) were all run by the ex-CIA, soldiers, mercs," he informed Murtaugh. "This is big business, Roger."

Mel wanted to know more about the background at the time, and when a script called *Air America* came in to him a year or so later, he became very interested.

"Most Americans knew nothing about that aspect of the Vietnam conflict," he said, when considering the script for his next film.

At the beginning then, there was a theme of authenticity about this property, which attracted the principals. Furthermore, the story was based on a serious, well-researched investigative book, called "Air America," written by British journalist, Christopher Robbins. The book exposed the clandestine, nefarious CIA operations, which included mass murder and dealings in the heroin trade — in fact anything, which would eliminate communism and the Viet Cong. Making likeable characters out of Air America people was going to be tricky, unless the facts were not allowed to get in the way of good fantasy.

Mel was originally signed to play a young pilot. In reality the fliers were unattractive, gung-ho types, who often hooked themselves on the drugs with which they dealt. Mel, perhaps shrewdly, switched to the role of an older pilot, Gene Ryack, a battle-fatigued, cynical operator, who wants to quit the company — Air America — and retire to live with the Laotians. The younger man's role went to stocky young Robert Downey Jr. and the director was Roger Spottiswoode.

Mel's asking price for the part moved up another million or two to the $5 to $7 million range, again with the mandatory points, which would only mean extra money if the film was huge. The budget of $35 million was middle range for the early 1990s when compared with the $100 million budget for the *Terminator* sequel.

A script was adapted, and in February 1990, a Hollywood film army reminiscent of that which made *Apocalypse Now* in the Philippines, was airlifted to Northern Thailand. There were twenty cameras, three units, a crew of more than five hundred, thirty planes and helicopters rented from the Thai military.

It was the second time Mel had ventured into Asia to make a movie, the first time being in late 1979 and early 1980 on *Attack Force Z*. Back then he was on a small salary and was hardly known anywhere in the Far East. Although Mad Max had hit cinemas in the West in 1979, the movie had yet to do the circuit in Japan and the rest of Asia (and to become a highly successful cult movie, especially in Japan).

Mel was then just another white face in a sea of two billion Asians. Now, a decade later he was THE white face, not just in Bangkok, where Mel was hounded for autographs, but also in the remote hill country region of Northern Thailand.

"No one knew my name," Mel said, "but they knew me as Mad Mack! It really surprised me."

Even the mighty opium warlord, Khun Sa, had a collection of *Mad Max* tapes and he was a big Mel Gibson fan, which was most useful to the *Air America* production. In exchange for an autograph from Mel, Khun Sa guaranteed that none of the Thai planes and choppers used in filming would be shot down. He did actually have the planes and hardware to carry out his threat should he have changed his mind. Nor would there be interference to the production. Khun Sa proved true to his word.

Mel kept up his reputation for clowning in the inevitable long waits between night scenes at the White Rose cafe in the town of Chiang Mai. He pretended to be a TV reporter in a restaurant.

"What brings you to Chiang Mai on a night like this?" Mel asked, putting a microphone under the noses of an unsuspecting American couple. They were stunned.

"Does your wife know you're here with this young woman?" Mel prompted.

"Hey," the woman said finally. "You're Mel Gibson."

"Yes I am."

Other tourists pulled out cameras and Mel posed with the couple.

"My daughter will never believe me," the man said, waving a menu, "unless you sign this."

Mel signed. It was proving to be a tough but enjoyable shoot and he was in a good mood, happy to be away from the backlots of Hollywood. He loved being treated as just another crew/cast member and eschewed the star treatment.

"I put it down to my background," Mel said, "and

you know, that Aussie thing of being part of a team. 'Cause that's what a good film is: a team effort. No one person makes that much difference, when you look at the total effort put in to make something work.''

Popular sentiments from honest, modest Mel, Superstar. However, despite his relaxed, good humour, the film to which he was giving his considerable skills and professionalism missed its mark. Perhaps it was because it wasn't a political film, while it was a highly-political subject. Or maybe because it had confused two styles — black comedy and fun exposé — with a serious backdrop.

The script had been conceived during the Vietnam conflict and finally drafted in 1977 and 1978. It had been through several re-writes via three directors — Richard Rush (*The Stunt Man*), Bob Rafelson and finally Spottiswoode.

He had taken it up after making *Under Fire* in 1984, which had been critical of American foreign policy in Nicaragua. Like many American directors, Spottiswoode wanted to interpret something new and definitive about Vietnam, and *Air America* seemed a more than adequate vehicle for this.

Unfortunately it ended as a pastiche — a sentimental MASH, with Mel as ever trying to ''lighten it up''. The final product was a featherweight film about a heavy subject. Not surprisingly author Christopher Robbins was appalled at the company's interpretation. They had made *Rambo* and *The Terminator* before.

''The film is a very trivial comedy about a tragedy,'' he told a London paper. ''A hundred thousand people were killed because of Air America's activities. How could you make such a book into a comedy?''

Mel wasn't going to supply answers. By the time he was doing post-production dubbing for *Air America,* his mind was firmly on lines from arguably history's finest writer in perhaps the finest work ever written in the English language: Hamlet.

CHAPTER

20

RIGGS DOES HAMLET

When Italian film director Franco Zeffirelli decided to attempt to film *Hamlet* he had thirty years of triumphs and failures in the industry to guide his decisions on just how he might do it. There were certain simple rules. It was important to have a big star play it to avoid a financial flop as far as possible. Zeffirelli's last big American film of a decade earlier — *Endless Love* with Brooke Shields — was a production with a very low-key ending and was a bomb. At sixty-eight years of age, another detonation would surely cause his demise as a Hollywood movie-maker.

Another rule was to make the star perform in a popular, attractive way. Zeffirelli was determined to make the chosen star a macho character, not a wimp, because putting derrieres on seats would be tough enough in the Mid-West or even the West-End when dealing with such a distinguished literary work. Traditionally the Danish Prince had been played as effete. As Zeffirelli put it, as "a little ballerina with white shirt and long blond hair and a black cloak." Layers of different theatrical cultures playing Hamlet over four centuries had misshapen and misrepresented Shakespeare's original inspiration until the character had become "this kind of idealized, contemplative, self-masturbatory queen. In the end women played him: Sarah Bernhardt, even Greta Garbo wanted to do it. He became a melancholic wimp.

"A man with tremendous power can still have doubts about his existence. Schwarzenegger I'm sure is afraid of death and of contemplation of "to be or not to be". So I began to think it was time to present Hamlet as he was, the way Elizabethan Man was: as a full-powered man, aggressive, threatening, difficult, capable of loving and hating. And strong. Hamlet was a Prince. He was the best man in the Kingdom. He was brought up to be king. The fact that he does not want to do anything with his power is because he has problems as a modern man." There have, of course, been fiercely masculine Hamlets. Those of Nicol Williamson, Albert Finney and Richard Burton spring to mind. But none of their interpretations were as coarsely aggressive as Mel's and none had the commercial, youthful, almost punkish truculence that Mel bought to the part. His was a brutal Prince, raw and uncompromising.

In *Hamlet,* Zeffirelli was tackling something from great experience which he felt certain he could do well. He had first directed the play for the US stage in 1964, as well as many productions in French and Italian. He tried to do another stage production in Los Angeles in 1979, starring Richard Gere, but it never got off the ground. Yet always lurking in the back of Zeffirelli's mind was the urge to put it on the big screen. He had put Shakespeare there before with *The Taming of the Shrew* (1967) featuring Elizabeth Taylor and Richard Burton, not to forget his classic elegiac version of *Romeo and Juliet* (which had grossed more than $130 million), or his cheeky *Otello,* in which he had dropped Desdemona's Willow Song in order to hasten the murder.

Having made the decision to go for Hamlet again, he set about choosing the star. The choice was limited. Jack Nicholson and Sean Connery came to mind because they had the right kind of masculinity, flair and skill but they were quickly dismissed as too old. Then there was De Niro, but had he the right look and would his voice stand it? Sure Bobby could do just about anything and Franco loved his fellow Italian, but it didn't seem to fit. In any case, he was lined up for two years on other projects . . .

Then there was Timothy Hutton. Not as big at the box-office as the others, but a wonderful actor. The director worried however, that he might have drifted into a conventional Hamlet, the sad, pensive prince. Zeffirelli was determined to obtain a bizarre, devilish character, "a man of the moment, a guy who fences better than anybody else, who rides better, who writes music and poetry — a complete Renaissance Man."

Yet there weren't that many of them about. Then the director's agent, Ed Limato, mentioned perhaps he should look at Mel Gibson, another of his clients. Attempting such links had obvious advantages and Limato was always on the lookout for opportunities with his star names, who included Michelle Pfeiffer, Richard Gere, Nicolas Cage, Alan Bates, Elizabeth McGovern, Michael York and Mathew Modine. Zeffirelli took himself off to see *Mad Max, Gallipoli* and *Lethal Weapon. Mad Max* particularly turned Franco on to Mel. "I responded to the energy, the violence, the danger of this character and it made me think of him a bit as an Elizabethan character: burning, threatening, vital. He wasn't that beautiful, but he was magnificent."

In the violent *Lethal Weapon* too, Zeffirelli, saw more of what he thought Shakespeare wanted four hundred years ago. There was a touch more of Shakespeare's "though this be madness, yet there is method in it".

In the suicidal scene, Gibson sticks a gun in his mouth and fingers the trigger. Zeffirelli claims to have cried to himself in the dark, "to be or not to be."

"Mel showed statue as a great tragedian, and more and more he loomed as the Dane."

The director tossed the idea around with friends and

was ridiculed. In the past they had called him difficult and eccentric. Now it was his age. "They thought I was senile," he recalled, "and that Father Time had caught up with me."

But the director knew his own mind. He met with Gibson's agent, who was now circumspect and advised Mel not to do it. Mel's first reaction was to concur.

"No way did I want to do this chestnut," he said. "A modern audience can't even understand Shakespeare's lines. And why court comparisons with Olivier! I could only lose. Then too, at the terms offered, I'd practically be doin' a freebie. On top of that I'd made four pictures in a row."

Yet still he was intrigued by the approach. His thoughts went back to those vital three minutes in 1975 when he auditioned for a place at NIDA with Edmund's speech in King Lear. Fresh in his mind also was the Bard training and the performances as Romeo opposite Judy Davis's Juliet at NIDA and then later at the Nimrod Theatre. Had he really come so far, so quickly, that he could even contemplate taking on Hamlet?

Mel did what Franco had done and spoke to mates about the role.

"You're putting your entire career on the line," one friend said a trifle melodramatically, "and for what? For a chance to become the biggest joke since the Edsel," referring to the "perfectly designed" 1950s American car that was the biggest consumer flop in automobile history.

Yet that was the point for Mel. The fact that he was even considering it would bring mirth to the media and it would demonstrate to the critics that he had something to prove. His professionalism was not limited to the mumbling Max or the reticent Riggs. He felt he had skills far beyond the journalist in *The Year of Living Dangerously* or the handicapped young man in *Tim*. But the reality was that those performances, which had been labelled with the much-hackneyed word "potential" were now a decade old. No matter how he saw and judged himself, the paying public, the media and even fellow professionals viewed him as restricted to roles in films such as *Lethal Weapon*.

Mel thought of Dustin Hoffman who had played Shylock in *The Merchant of Venice* on the London stage. Clearly he had taken that step to prove something to himself. Shakespeare was after all, the yardstick of being a professional and probably would be forever.

With this in mind he discussed it further with Limato. A lunch was arranged with Zeffirelli at the Four Seasons Hotel in Los Angeles. Mel read the script again with an eye for what it was to be Hamlet.

"It suddenly had a different significance from the play I'd been so aloof from in school," he recalled.

Mel chatted enthusiastically with Zeffirelli about the role. The director, always charming but using some craft, remarked:

"This role will be a never-ending Calvary, a damnation. Hamlet is infinite, an ocean of possibilities. You can drown in them. He can destroy you."

Mel slept on it and woke up as Mad Max, telling Limato that morning: "What the hell? Let's have a go. There's nothing quite like the exhilaration of putting your equipment on the chopping block."

He rang Zeffirelli and told him he would do it.

"I was determined I was gonna do my best," Mel

Mel said, "gonna have fun." But at first he felt it was a no-win situation, which was his way of dramatising the possibility of failure to psyche himself up. He was shored up by friends in the industry.

"I felt very positive about it," John Badham, who directed him in *Bird On A Wire,* said. "You'll give as much as any actor could."

Robert Downey, with perceptive irony, told him he would either get an Academy Award nomination or it "will be the second time Shakespeare ever grossed $100 million."

However, even with Mel signed up, it wasn't easy to raise the finance. $15.5 million was needed. In the end, Gibson's own company, Icon — which he had started with Australian accountant turned producer, Bruce Davey — put up a big slice of the budget. Mel was to be paid a million dollars (less than 20 per cent of what he got for *Air America*), plus a favourable percentage deal. Mel was convinced on paper, at least, that he could break even without too much difficulty. But to walk away without being a cent ahead was going to be a gamble, especially when you were competitive and conscious of the fact that the other big male superstars were now asking $10 million a picture, plus a percentage of the gross. The gamble and arguments from those who were for the deal were that first, a big commercial action *Hamlet* could be box-office. And second, that Mel could move ahead of the big name pack by a top performance. He could ask $10 million a picture after Hamlet, he was told, because the studios would then be convinced he had an extra acting dimension. *Hamlet* would demonstrate he could take on just about anything and succeed. Still all the optimism was reduced to facts. Mel now not only had his future on the line, his money was there too.

Anxiety soon set in. The tabloids worldwide chuckled at the news with headlines such as: "Mad Max to Play Crazy Dane," and "Mel To Ham It With Hamlet", which he took phlegmatically enough. After all, he had just come off three pictures back-to-back — *Lethal Weapon II, Bird On A Wire* and *Air America,* which the purists, art-house critics and true Shakesperians would have to brand broadly as trashy. He decided to use the cynicism and doubting remarks as a spur. Mel was determined to broaden and deepen his reputation as an actor.

Then he heard about Daniel Day Lewis, who had gone into a nervous collapse over the role of Hamlet, and had been forced to abandon it. Mel read the play ten times in a week. The more he read the more edgy he became. He told fellow actors that he felt like a "barbarian" tackling Shakespeare but this was probably to cover himself in case he flopped. Yet he had threads to cling to. He had proved himself in a variety of roles on film and he had had a go at Shakespeare as Romeo. He had tackled that tricky language and not just read it. Still, he couldn't placate his inner insecurity.

"So many ways to do it, none of them safe. Contradictions everywhere. Nasty twists an turns. Hellish! And on top of that those incredible, great, fine lines. Shakespeare serves ace after ace and I don't know how to whack 'em back," he said.

Mel consulted an English professor, who guided him to "about twenty-five" books of critique — some for schools and others for professionals. This served partly to confuse, for each author presented Hamlet in a different manner.

"In the end I just gave up trying to find the real character," he said later. "I thought I'd do my best and that would have to do."

He decided to concentrate on the text and make his own interpretation. Mel developed a modern view, which still lined up with the director's vision of what Shakespeare was initially seeking. His memory of how he began to see Hamlet and the play is instructive, because it supported Zeffirelli's decision to offer him the role.

"What Hamlet can't do is stop worrying. He's more than worried. He's having a breakdown. Okay, he gets this terrible news. His father's just died. He held him in very high regard. I mean, every time he talks about him it's as though he were some god, and perhaps his reverence has grown since he died. And what really irks him is that this other fella, Claudius, has married his mother and taken his place as King. Why he should have it and not Hamlet, I don't know. He has come back and his uncle has quite rightly stepped into the position, because the place will be in disarray if he doesn't act quickly.

"He can't make up his mind because his mind is infected. There's something stopping him. He's distracted. He must be totally distracted the whole time. Then he has these flashes of brilliance. His strong points are the things that tie him up. That's the tragedy. His intelligence. His way of reasoning. They seem to be the things that weigh him down. He reflects too much.

"Hamlet is in one hell of a flummox. He's a man of action, but he can't act. He knows Claudius killed his dad, but he can't come to terms with it. Even after he has the evidence, he keeps running in circles. He plays word games. He pretends to be crazy. In parallel with this his emotions build up and up. Then Kaboom! The volcano erupts — but at the wrong time and over the wrong guys.

"He calls his mother a whore. He breaks Ophelia's heart. He bumps off Polonius, a harmless old fool, and he doesn't give a damn.

"He's a minefield of contradictions and ambiguities and can be both acutely sensitive and brutally cruel, and he has no sense of proportion or timing. Hamlet can be rational, yet volatile. The man was a livin' time bomb and that's how I decided to play him."

More than shades of Martin Riggs and Fletcher Christian. In fact, at times, of Mel Gibson himself.

The actor rented a house in Hertfordshire with Robyn and the six kids and prepared for the pivotal role of his career. Someone, he had forgotten who, told him to prepare his voice as if he was in training for a sixteen round heavyweight title fight, for it was the vocal chords supported by the lungs that would make or break him. Physical strength is important in tackling any demanding play. A performer couldn't afford to pause for breath in the middle of a long thought. It could destroy meaning.

Zeffirelli suggested he increase his lung capacity and that meant the Marlboro man had to quit cigarettes. Then he went to work with vocal coach Julia Wilson-Dickinson for forty hours a week to build up his wind. Eight weeks on, he had lifted his lung capacity by a quarter. In parallel, he had to work on his voice and transfer oceans from the hybrid mid-Pacific Aussie-American to something else.

"I didn't want to be a clipped Noel Coward or even too English," Mel explained. "I wanted a sound and fluency right for a Prince with kingly aspirations.''

Zeffirelli and Mel also worked assiduously at cultivating a distinctive look for Hamlet. Tradition had made him the velvet intellectual, but this was never going to be Mel, either in effeminate gear or as the deep thinker. Costume designers, hairdressers and make-up artists came up with the short-haired (lightly tinted and flattened), rough-bearded Viking in coarse woollen tunic and leggings, described by one of them as "the dangerous, painful, maneless Dane.'' Even the uncomfortable boots that wardrobe found for him, caused an uneven gait, which he liked. It all helped Mel get a grip on the character.

There were also more practical matters to attend to. Mel had fencing scenes so he had to learn the ancient art. He also had sequences on horseback so he had to learn to ride which surprised a few people in the production. Despite Mel owning cattle ranches he had not had to ride before. There were managers and hired hands to do that. Besides, rounding up cattle is done with four-wheel drive vehicles or even planes on modern ranches. Meanwhile the director was busy redrafting the script with screen writer Christopher De Vore. They edited down several scenes before filming rather than shoot them, only to abandon them on the cutting-room floor.

"I couldn't afford to do a big, expensive scene only to cut it if it didn't work out," Zeffirelli recalled.

Cut back were scenes and speeches such as those concerning the ill-fated Rosencrantz and Guildenstern, who appear only in a few scenes. Contentiously Zeffirelli did not think these characters deserved more air.

He was not intimidated by certain speeches beloved by actors and audiences and they too received the knife.

He justified the film surgery by saying that Shakespeare's worldwide fame with people of different cultures, languages and backgrounds was derived from the stories and the characters.

Zeffirelli began signing up the rest of the talent. And what talent was there to give the production ballast: Alan Bates as Claudius, Paul Scofield as the ghost of Hamlet's father, Ian Holm as Polonius, Helena Bonham-Carter as Ophelia, and Glenn Close as Gertrude.

Before shooting started, Mel and the senior British performers — Scofield, Bates and Holm, met for lunch. The discussion turned to the great Hamlets portrayed by Laurence Olivier, John Gielgud, Alec Guinness, Derek Jacobi and Nicol Williamson. All present except for Mel had played Hamlet and were recognized as being in the top bracket of stage and screen actors in the English language. They spoke with eloquence and clarity in layers that Mel had only scratched at. They listened, politely and encouragingly to his offerings, but he started feeling doubtful about his capacity to scale the theatre world's Everest. Bates remarked that he thought it was the greatest role in literature, and Holm thought it the toughest, and this was from men representative of an acting tradition that thought starving with a provincial repertory company or working at the Shakespeare Memorial Theatre in Stratford-upon-Avon, was commendable, if not a pre-requisite for playing Hamlet.

Typically, Mel got something out of the lunch apart from a touch of the inferiorities. Ian Holm had run on with a soliloquy or two and Mel noticed the value he was getting from enunciating consonants and he realized he was getting a little slack here. It was a bad habit from American films where naturalism (sometimes a euphemism for sloppiness), is emphasized to the nth degree. This was not place for sloppy language from sloppy actors for a sloppy audience. He was now in a league where the script was from the most gifted writer in history, where the parts demanded the finest acting and where the audience would demand, not bubble-gum for the mind, but powerful intellectual nourishment. Thus Mel worked even harder on his voice.

He didn't actually find an accent until just before the beginning of the shoot, which was to range in location from Shepperton Studios to castles along the coasts of Kent and Scotland. Mel walked onto the set on the first day at the granite Dover Castle, having done painstaking preparation in the family atmosphere — even his parents Hutton and Anne were flown out from Australia.

Still, it was a tough start. His first scene was a writhing soliloquy that dipped into self-hate (*I am pidgeon-livered and lack gall to make oppression bitter*) then strode through a cunning claim (*I'll have these players play something like the murder of my father before mine uncle . . . if he but belch . . .*), lifted to anger (*Bloody, bawdy villain!*) and finished with calm and thoughtful decision (*The play's the thing wherein I'll catch the conscience of the king*).

Like a determined mountain-climber, Mel attacked the rock. Take one, two and three. The director called for a break and discussed the scene, never patronising, always softly encouraging, occasionally calling someone darling, but never Mel, who was not a man on which such a theatrical endearment settled easily.

Near the end of the day, Mel asked Zeffirelli what he thought about the work in progress.

"It has the right feel, we're coming well," he said with a smile. He could see that his star was fatigued.

"Had enough?" the director asked.

"Not unless you have," replied Mel. Zeffirelli called a halt, and Mel was relieved. He disappeared into his dressing room, where a friend handed him a present. Mel opened the box and in it found an elegant hand-stitched shirt.

"It had a blood-stain on the right sleeve," Mel recalled, "and I was told it had been worn by Larry Olivier in his great film adaptation of *Hamlet*. I was urged to put it on there and then, but I waited until I was alone in my hotel room before I did. You hear about such things givin' you good luck and all that. It fitted, but it didn't feel right. Know what I mean? I hadn't had a day I'd liked. I was feeling unsatisfied. I'd been maybe too pent up for it and I wasn't in the mood for superstitions so I took that shirt off and put it back in the box. I'm me. Larry's Larry. I had to do it my way." Fair enough, but Mel Gibson is now in possession of one of the greatest of theatre icons. We can only assume that he cherishes it.

Perhaps the most exciting and atmospheric location was Dunnottar Castle. Sitting majestically on a craggy outcrop on Scotland's east coast, it became Elsinore, and it was here that Mel and the *Hamlet* company took on the gravedigger scene, with cruel April winds biting at them. The director now moved up a few gears in an effort to shove four weeks work into two, demanding that Mel act all day. At night he hid in his bedroom, learning the next day's lines.

"He always shows great courage and energy," Holm told reporters during shooting. "By that I mean grace under pressure."

The climax was the famous skull soliloquy, where Hamlet, tormented intellectual, contemplates his own death.

"It was strange watching Zeffirelli, one one side of the skull and Gibson, face down in the dirt on the other side, going through take after take on this vital sequence," said French journalist, Jacques Le Grossman, representing several French magazines. "I thought Mel got it right in many takes, but he and the director were looking, I guess, for perfection."

In the end, Mel gave a smooth yet sensitive interpretation of some of the most hackneyed lines in literary history: *Alas, poor Yorick! I knew him well . . . Horatio, a fellow of infinite jest . . . He hath borne me on his back a thousand times . . . Where be your gibes now? Your gambols? Your songs? . . . Now get you to my lady's chamber, and tell her, let her paint, let her paint an inch thick, to this favour she must come; make her laugh at that.*

After about take nine and many breaks, Zeffirelli scrambled up from the damp grass and called, "that's the one . . . print it."

"Happy?" asked Mel, eyebrows raised.

"You're coming along," Zeffirelli said.

Mel beamed and picked up the skull, feigning as if to kick it towards a goal . . .

Shooting in Scotland took a lot out of Mel and he was hindered by a bad back.

"It was the horse they gave me for those riding scenes," he complained. "It ran on rocket fuel and jarred my ageing frame."

The production returned to Shepperton Studios, outside London where most of the big remaining scenes would be shot. Mel retired for a quick break at the farm he rented for Robyn and the kids.

"I sort of recuperated mentally and physically," he told reporters. "I got fit taking walks with Robyn and lifting babies. After a few days I was ready to tackle the end of Hamlet. Very emotional stuff."

It was an explosive, violent confrontation between the hero and his mother. It was the scene they had to get "right", yet the director wanted something different, something memorable and audacious. Glenn Close and Mel did too. The three agreed that Hamlet's feelings for his mother were incestuous, and that the strong attraction was reciprocated. Zeffirelli had cast these two partly for their great screen physicality. This was the moment to use it in combination to the production's advantage. He urged them to come up with something that would present Hamlet's reaction as a hybrid of a sublimated murder instinct and eroticism.

Having bullocked his way through a grinding schedule, mainly because of the modest budget, now told them. "We must make this work, no matter how long it takes."

For a while it seemed it would never succeed and both the performers agreed it was the toughest scene they had ever shot in combined careers that covered more than thirty years.

"Nothing in *Max* or *Gallipoli* or *LW* was ever as rugged as this," Mel told Le Grossman.

"It was just plain brutal," Close said. "The most difficult scene. And it was hot. Our costumes were wool. I acknowledged that the fibre breathes better than others, but we were under powerful stage lamps and the set was tiny. We both sweated because the scene was tough and on top of that it could have been the Sahara."

The trio struggled for nearly five days and by the end of day two they were near-exhausted.

"I was so fatigued," Close recalls, "I just flopped on the floor between shots and takes. I had to weep every take. I must have wept for twelve hours. Oh, it was wonderful! I felt totally cleansed."

Ian Holm was so inspired during the moment when Close tries to escape the confrontation, that he took Mel aside and suggested quietly that he break with convention and not grab her as Hamlets had done for four centuries.

"Why not grunt or whistle?" he said. "A noise might just do it."

Mel grinned. He liked the idea. Close ran for the door and Mel let go a howl like a wolf.

Hamlet flings the Queen on her bed and leaps on top of her at the height of the incestuous charade.

"Oh Hamlet!" she implores, "speak no more!"

But the Prince seems out of control now and he is propelled by a lustful rage. Mouth contorted in disgust he violently thrusts his loins, simulating the incest he believes she has committed and he appears to desire.

Later Mel claimed a lot of people were shaken by that scene. He and Close were amongst them.

"It took me a while to get over the nightmares about it," Close said.

Yet it was this scene above all that persuaded his peers that Gibson had reached a Hamlet pinnacle.

"It wasn't just that incest scene," Close remarked later, "but in general Mel plays with great sexiness and vigor. He's also an incredibly passionate Hamlet, and most importantly he's an accessible Hamlet. Millions will understand him for the first time."

Alan Bates was genuinely effusive and generous in his praise: "Mel's playing is utterly truthful and I think quite wonderful." Ian Holm was also happy to call Gibson a worthy Hamlet.

"He was terrific," he noted. "Very physical, tremendously vital."

With shooting complete, Zeffirelli began the task of overseeing the edit and the reduction of the play from its original four and a half hours.

"We've got to aim at two hours," he told Mel.

"Oh, Jesus, two hours out!"

"No. The completed version must be two."

Mel was stunned and then horrified as the edit began.

"Franco and I went through it," Mel recalls, and he sat in the editing room, mortified as the slashing began.

"Oh, no, please Franco, not that scene, not that soliloquy!" he said more times than he would like to recall. But the director pillaged the performance. A cut there, a complete sequence removed here.

"I was just bleeding," Mel says, " 'Oh, God, no Franco you can't cut the rest of that' — all that kind of stuff. But I began to see that what was left was working OK.''

Zeffirelli kept reminding him that there would always be a long version for scholars one day in the future to review. They would have it all for their personal pleasure and for posterity.

In the end even Zeffirelli couldn't stand to cut any more and the final product ran two hours and twenty minutes. Distributors would have to live with it.

"He fooled with the adaptations a little,'' Mel observed, "but I don't think we offended the purists, but we have taken some licence. That's inevitable when you're taking a great, great play to the screen. But remember, there's no absolute right way to do it, considering too that we have to open it out for film.''

Asked by the journalist Le Grossman what Shakespeare would have thought, Mel pondered for a moment.

"Ah, Jesus,'' he replied, "Shakespeare would have been turned on by film. As for Hamlet, you wonder what he would have done with it, or any of his works for that matter.''

Zeffirelli and Mel were quietly optimistic that their five-month production was nothing if not courageous. The director cut the opening scene entirely and began instead with the funeral of Hamlet's father.

"Everything flows from this, Zeffirelli explained. "You have all the key players introduced and involved. It has momentum from then on . . .''

The king is mourned by Gertrude and his uncle, Claudius who turns to Hamlet and says: *Think of us as a father* . . .

Zeffirelli wanted to make Hamlet's swagger and aggression stand out, so he eliminated the character of Fortinbras.

"He, Fortinbras, has traditionally been seen as the contrast to the cautious, nail-biting Hamlet," he explained. In removing him the story is relieved of its political emphasis too. It becomes a family tragedy more than a political one."

The director's emotional highlight is Hamlet's feeling of betrayal by his mother. Coupled with this, Hamlet knows of the crime, his father's murder, of which everyone else seems ignorant. He can't really say his father's ghost informed him, but he must somehow bring the crime into the open, but how?

As the story unfolds we see the great clash of cunning and drive between Hamlet and Claudius. Hamlet tries to lead his Uncle along, by pretending to be insane and then putting on a play that is meant to expose and incriminate Claudius before the entire court.

Yet Claudius has his own schemes to break Hamlet. The Prince's "friends" are sent to spy on him, and then Claudius sends his nephew off to England with secret orders for his assassination. The director built this clash of guile and style well until the duel scene when the dirty deeds that Claudius has created ensnare him.

Zeffirelli's choice of Mel was never so poignant as when Hamlet becomes the avenger, even if what he is avenging is his own psychological wounds — the emotional damage done to him within the family. Mel as the mad, cruel schemer is convincing, and it was this that turned the director on to Mel in *Mad Max* and Martin Rigg in *Lethal Weapon*. Mel proves the master at playing the guy hurting inside; the man with the explosive nature hidden behind a thin veil of controlled mania.

In the "To be or not to be" and "Alas, Poor Yorick," scenes this Hamlet gives the impression that he is stirred by his own surprising ideas, rather than a cogitating Prince holding the stage for a reflective moment. For Mel, thoughtful interludes are like a distance runner pausing to be   refreshed   by   a flask of water, rather than someone stopping for a meal.

Mel's wariness and jumpiness in the early scenes radiate and reflect his inner turmoil. This of course, is a consequence of what is generated on the big screen with sharp cutting, close ups and different angles. It is a classic example of modern movie-making. Other screen Hamlets of decades earlier would be positively pedestrian compared to Zeffirelli's enlivening the character and the subject with all the film technology and skills at his disposal.

For a while Mel's Hamlet remains the prowling tiger, on the outskirts of the action in the colourful court. He watches disdainfully as Polonius advises his daughter, and disgustedly as Claudius banquets on, as if assessing his future prey.

Later in the duel scene with Laertes — a contest which Claudius has set up to kill Hamlet — Mel takes those risks for which he is becoming famous. There is a touch of the crazy Martin Riggs with his Three Stooges bluff. There is also a little taste of Fletcher Christian acting hysterically and letting the strange side of his character loose after the mutiny in *The Bounty*.

In all three instances, the viewer is left uncertain of whether he is performing like a lunatic to unsettle his foes, or if he really is a lunatic who has lost control.

Hamlet looks over-confident as he winks at his mother during the duel. What is the audience to ponder? That Hamlet is wild? Foolhardy? Fatalistic? The hero totally in command? It matters little, for the effect is in keeping with the character. Even the heavy broadswords that are used in the duel scene have a realism beyond the image conjured by mere fencing foils, and give the impression that the Prince is toying with, and teasing death.

This triumph of Mel, the controlled loon, is evident in other scenes such as the moment when he asks Ophelia where her father is, knowing full well he is spying on him at that moment.

"Her answer of 'at home my Lord,' sets Hamlet off again as he attempts to fool the spies into believing he is the full, certifiable idiot.

Throughout, Mel is supported by superb performances by Alan Bates, Ian Holm, Paul Scofield as an imposing ghost, and Helena Bonham-Carter.

Zeffirelli sought more emotion and earthiness along with far more action than earlier cinematic renditions of *Hamlet,* such as Grigori Kozintsev's suitably political and bleak Soviet version (1964), and Olivier's witty, black version (1948). Shakespeare is more sophisticated and subtle than this latest effort, yet adaptations are about interpretation and Zeffirelli provided a vehicle for Mel which has suspense and pace that grabs, while not turning from the sex and violence that is woven into most of today's filmic extravaganzas.

Confident of the final version, Mel threw himself into a world promotional tour with unprecedented relish. He had never been one for publicity or the media, but this time his reputation and his own money were involved. There was little he could do about the critics. Yet he could try to personally reach the movie-goers, who fell into two camps. There was the tiny minority that knew and loved Hamlet and would go and see it even if the film was laughed out of town by the critics. Then there was the great mass of ordinary film lovers, who would normally ignore a classic adaptation. For these, if Mel, a mass box-office star, was willing to promote it enthusiastically, then perhaps it would be worth a look.

With *Lethal Weapon* and other films he had, albeit reluctantly, done what was expected of him in pushing the movie. But often it didn't matter because his name on anything short of a turkey was going to pull them in. *Hamlet* was different and needed nearly as much effort in the promotion as in the making.

An educational video on *Hamlet* was made as part of the push. It was shot with Mel and students of University High in Los Angeles. He talked to them in language they were familiar with.

"The story is great. . . it has eight violent deaths, murder, incest, adultery, a mad woman, poison, revenge, humour . . . and sword fights . . ."

The students were not studying literature and they said they would normally have steered clear of anything so upmarket as Shakespeare, movie or play. But Mel had whetted their appetites with a lot of intriguing questions and they all wanted to see the movie. It was encouraging to him, too, for he realised that if he could enthuse a young audience he and Zeffirelli would succeed in making the Shakespearean play as popular as any show in town, something, it could be argued, which had not been done since the sixteenth century.

Mel started fronting the media and always to packed conferences because it was a rare event to have him eager to talk to show business reporters. They tried to sidetrack him about just about everything but *Hamlet,* but he managed to get in the right plugs.

Then just before the film's premier, he received a phone call from Australia. His mother, Anne, who had been ill with diabetes and a heart condition, had died.

Mel, in shock, caught the first available plane for Australia. It took twenty-four hours and he had time to reflect and face reality. He told friends later that he couldn't sleep on the plane and he started smoking again. He saw some tragic irony in the fact that he had just spent five months in a production that had dwelt on a relationship between mother and son, in which he had thought constantly about Anne and how much he owed her.

Mel was deeply disapointed too in the sudden knowledge that she would never see his *Hamlet.* She had always been proud over his phenomenal success in life, and he understood more than anyone that it was due in no small measure to his parents. They had given him a solid base of values for life. Sure, he had strayed from them often enough, but because they had been instilled into him and his siblings, he always had a moral compass. Not only had these values given him a sense of direction, they had helped him keep it when he was rocketed into Hollywood's stratosphere.

Mel had become a great star. He had the self-assurance to to match the best purely on looks and physique. He had the personality and drive to match the most driven and energetic and he had the intelligence and gifts that were now allowing him to be at least compared with some of the great actors of the era. These attributes came along with the luck of timing. Had the Australian film industry not emerged in the late 1960s, there would have been no support for a *Mad Max, Gallipoli* or *Year of Living Dangerously* produced so well in a fledgling industry, and Mel would never had been heard of. No one in his family was going to pull strings that would have seen him given a chance in Hollywood. There wasn't a rich father or uncle who would have financed him in New York or London. Mel was first to acknowledge that his rise from obscurity was a beneficiary of timing. But Anne and Hutton had given honest love, and a stable family, which could never be bought and once attained never lost.

So when he first found it difficult to cope with the demands of work and global fame that came in the mid-1980s, he always had family to return to for normality.

To Anne Gibson, he was always just funny little Mel, nothing special amongst the kids, but always loved in an unlimited and unqualified way. Now she was gone, and Mel felt a little cheated and bitter. He was never quite sure how his mother felt about the movies that had made him big. He doubted she would ever have gone to a cinema to see a *Mad Max* or a *Lethal Weapon* without Mel in it. But he knew she would probably have watched *Hamlet*. Anne Gibson would have approved.

Mel arrived home in the Kiewa Valley, which immediately shut down around its most celebrated inhabitant in his time of grief. The townsfolk would make sure that no unwelcome reporter would creep into the area, because they looked after their own and Mel was one of them. He was not Mel Gibson superstar, but Mel Gibson local farmer. In addition, there was respect for Anne and Hutton, who had been admired members of the local community — honest, Godfearing and generous. Good country folk. Now one of them had died and the locals would pay their respects.

But Mel did not stay in the valley long after the funeral. He did what he thought his mother would want and returned to Los Angeles to give everything to *Hamlet*'s success.

Warner Bros was distributing the movie and their executives warned reporters at the first media conference not to mention Anne's death, or even offer condolences. Mel was dressed sombrely in a black suit over a black and beige polo shirt. He clutched a packet of Marlboro and looked like the nervous old Mel who hated those other perfunctory, mandatory conferences with previous films. The tension was eased marginally as the questions started.

Would he like to tackle more Shakespeare? Would he like to play King Lear for example?

"Maybe, up the track, yeah it's possible," Mel replied laconically and without conviction.

What was it like to have Glenn Close, who at forty-three was not much older than him, playing his mother?

Before the end of the question the room fell silent. Mel dragged on a cigarette.

"It was fantastic," he said. "She was so good I think I'll adopt her."

There were a few polite, nervous smiles at the answer which was full of quiet pathos and poignancy. The tension went up a notch as Mel added uncertainly, "she's great to work with, but young to be my mother,'' before his voice trailed off.

Mel was not looking for sympathy personally or professionally and he knew he was not about to get any from the critics, who slumped in dingy preview cinemas across the U.S., where *Hamlet* was first released. For the first time in his career, Mel was very eager to read all reviews. The most influential critic in the USA was Vincent Canby of the *New York Times,* which had long been the instant maker or breaker for plays, and as this was an adaptation of one of the great plays in history by the greatest director ever, the *Times* view would have an important effect on the movie version.

The paper said, ''Mel Gibson's Hamlet is strong, intelligent and safely beyond ridicule,'' which demonstrated the surprise that the critical intelligensia viewed Mel even trying the role. It justified his courage in having a go, because unless he did he would forever be branded with *Lethal Weapons* that would keep him safely within ridicule.

''He is a visceral Hamlet,'' the *Times* reviewer went on, ''tortured by his own thoughts and passions, confused by his recognition of evil, a Hamlet whose emotions are raw, yet who retains the desperate wit to act mad. He is by far the best part of Zeffirelli's sometimes slick but always lucid and beautifully cinematic version of the play.''

This review was consistent with other U.S. papers, such as the big selling national *USA Today,* which trumpeted: ''It's a triumph few could have predicted . . .'' Another hint to Mel that the man who played Martin Riggs was a shock to many as a startlingly good actor.

The *New York Times* continued the marginally

patronising line by remarking that "those who come to mock this strutting Hollywood player may be surprised by his vigorous self-assured performance."

The *New York Post* was honest and less patronising when it commented: "Yes, Mel Gibson makes a very good Hamlet. By my troth, a very, very good Hamlet, and it's a doubly pleasant surprise, since all we've had to judge him by are the likes of *Mad Max* and *Lethal Weapon,* in which dilemmas are most easily resolved with fisticuffs than with soliloquy . . ."

Equally direct was the *Toronto Globe and Mail.*

"Okay, let's get the obvious question out of the way first," it said. "Mel Gibson cast as Hamlet? You bet, and he's just fine, thank you. Not stellar or definitive, but entirely of a piece with what is a defiantly cinematic reading of the play . . ."

Most of the important U.S. magazines and papers were similar in their surprised praise and this indicated it could do well at the box-office. Warner Bros would have liked someone to have the courage to have reviewed it without trying to air their knowledge of Shakespeare, but all the critics seemed bent on playing it straight. As one executive put it:

"We would have loved someone to have said, "This story is a big action movie set in the sixteenth-century about a Prince who is out for revenge against his father's killer. The King's court is against him . . . etcetera . . . the acting is superb, the script by a little known writer is promising . . ." Everytime someone mentions "the greatest play in English literature" or "a classic", or "the most difficult part in theatre", I cringe. Of course, we can never overcome the language. The choice of Mel by

Franco was inspired, because his body language and vigour go some way to making the soliliquies and speeches intelligible to a modern audience.''

Mel returned to Australia in 1991 for *Hamlet*'s release. He visited NIDA, where the Mel Gibson-Village Roadshow-NIDA scholarship for a creative or technical student was announced. It was worth $100,000. He spoke to students again and was greeted as a real hero rather than a celluloid one. He was a world-famous performer who had shown a great range by tackling the classics and succeeded. Mel had helped put NIDA on the map. It could now point to Mel and Judy Davis as worldbeating examples of the school's output. Producers in all countries would now consider NIDA graduates more seriously.

The audience of students were eager to ask questions and Mel, looking tanned and fit in a cream suit, was in good form, back to his horsing around and double entendres. He told his publicity minder that the steaks he ate at home came from his own cattle, and when she, slightly put off, asked what it was like to eat his own animals, Mel replied: ''noisy.''

His expressions were as mobile as ever. The Groucho Marx use of the eyebrows, wacky expressions and European use of the hands to make a point were in full swing from the opening question.

''Is Hamlet your best role?'' one novice asked.

''No, my next one will be. Except if I'm Daffy Duck.''

''Will you be haunted by Hamlet?'' another asked.

''You mean because of his torment?''

''Yeah, you know, actors have said it never leaves you.''

"I'm not going to let the bugger bother me," Mel replied, pulling a comic expression.

"I know you've had good reviews," another student began, "but how did you feel when the tabloids first heard you would play Hamlet? They were a bit demeaning . . ."

"Who cares?" Mel responded. "I don't. I'm rich."

That brought a big cheer. Many young actors dreamt of being so successful that they could ignore the critics, especially those in the dreaded tabloids. Yet Mel was one of the few who could do it and get away with it without seeming arrogant and offensive.

"Did you think you got the Hamlet character the way you wanted it?"

"Hey, good question," Mel replies inoffensively mocking the tyro. "Who is that guy, Norman Gunston [a funny Aussie interviewer] or Mike Willessee [a well-known TV interviewer]? The answer is that the deeper I got into the role, the more I revised the original ideas on him [Hamlet]. I mean, things kept popping out of the woodwork at you. Sometimes it got so confusing that on the day you'd have to make a choice, and follow it through. But right up to that point — God, it was shifting. It's very difficult to draw a bead on that character. On stage it would be great because you could make different choices every night."

Did he give up smoking in order to add to his own creative tension, to indirectly intensify his portrayal of a tortured, tormented Hamlet?

Mel grimaced. "I don't believe in that school of acting," he said. "I don't enjoy it and I don't subscribe to it. I like to be natural — you know, joke around — right up to the time the camera rolls."

He was also asked what he thought of the Australian Actors Equity regulations on the importation of foreign actors in the local film and TV industry. Equity had been notoriously inequitable towards foreigners.

"Look, it's tougher today than it was for me," he replied, "but [Equity's] immovable rules were causing the industry to stagnate. I don't think that artistic endeavour should have any boundaries. I really don't. A lot of artists here — film directors and camera people — they don't have green cards, which allow permanent access to the U.S. and they work like mad in the states. They get them somehow. If you're good enough you'll end up working over there, so why should we exclude the rest of the world from working here?"

The remark brought a tepid response from the idolizing audience. Actors Equity were upset.

"Gibson's career was launched under the system that he now condemns," a miffed Equity spokesman pointed out. "Under his free-for-all rules he would not have been chosen for *Mad Max*. The producers most likely would have brought in an American actor instead of casting an unknown from NIDA."

It was an arguable point. The *Mad Max* budget was so small that the producers may well have been happy to cast the no-name Aussie anyway.

Later after the fun at NIDA, Mel sat at a table doodling on a pad while meeting four members of the national press. The questions got a little more irritating. Inevitably the violence issue was again raised.

"Do you feel you've contributed to the American mentality of invading countries by acting in movies featuring violence?" one scribe asked.

"What, in *Hamlet*?" Mel responded, barely containing his anger. He had just about had enough of this query.

"No with . . ."

"No," Mel replied crisply.

"But American studies have shown that certain films . . ."

"The others are certainly no more violent than *Hamlet* or some of those other Jacobbean tragedies." The queries and increasingly weary answers continued.

It was clear that he would rather be somewhere else and he was soon in another room giving a promised one-on-one interview with a reporter from *The Australian*. When asked if he was a "Creationist", in other words, believed that God created all life beginning with man.

"Yeah, I think I am. In Shakespearean terms it's a case of "to be or not to be", and we all ask ourselves that, don't we?" Mel then adroitly pulled it back to the conference, and didn't come up with answers. He just presents a lot of possibilities, but with a lot more style and poetry than most of us would."

"Does your faith help you with the big problems in life?" an interviewer asked, probing into areas that Mel had always been reluctant to speak about, since he regarded them as "private and personal".

"Sure it does," he replied uncomfortably, "Was I created? Did I evolve out of a piece of dirt or was there some kind of intelligence behind it? Why I'm here, how I function . . . I don't think it happened by accident."

A few days later, Mel arrived at a party reception at the cinema, which was to screen the Australian premier.

"There was no fanfare when he arrived," one guest observed. "He sort of fell in the door at the reception.

Someone offered him champagne, but he asked if he could have a beer. He lit a cigarette and mingled with the guests. He seemed totally himself, unpretentious. He was quick to shower praise on the other performers in *Hamlet*."

After an hour the guests began moving to the cinema. Mel disappeared upstairs, ignored seats reserved for VIPs and took an unreserved seat to the side. When the show was over and the lights went on, applause and cheering broke out and all heads turned towards Mel. But he was not there. He had slipped quietly out minutes before the end.

Mel again paid more attention than usual to what the critics had to say. Australia ranked about seventh in terms of markets for Mel's films, but this was home, and while the U.S. critics has been important for the financial success of the film, Australian critics were important to him personally. It was the home of knockers and he had experienced his share of attempts to "cut down the tall poppy," an Aussie tradition.

The Australian newspaper's Evan Williams, a tough critic of Mel's performances in the past, said:

"Having seen *Hamlet* I felt I should take back all the unkind things I've said about Mel Gibson over the years. He's done something brave and important . . . whether it's a performance that will live in the memory is harder to say. It may not haunt us the way Olivier's did, or match the great Derek Jacobi Hamlet . . . but it's a performance of considerable power and concentration; and if it ranks in the end as a very good Hamlet rather than a great one, the fault lies more with Zeffirelli than with Mel. For this is essentially a safe production, and for Zeffirelli an oddly cautious one . . . It's Gibson's film and so it should be.

And one or two moments have a touch of greatness. His Yorick speech in the graveyard may be the best I have heard; the closet scene with Gertrude has a potency that perhaps only Gibson (recently confirmed in a British poll as the world's number one sex symbol), could suggest. Hamlet's sigh after seeing the Ghost really is piteous and profound, and one of my tests for any Hamlet is how well he delivers that lovely line "Rest, rest, perturbed spirit". If he rushes or gabbles it, it loses its note of exhausted supplication, of a man already daunted by the task before him. Mel does it beautifully. I'm afraid it's a better performance than Zeffirelli deserves."

Neil Jillet, in the *Melbourne Age,* one of the country's most experienced and, at times scathing reviewers, pleasantly shocked even Mel.

"Gibson is a strong Hamlet, ruthless and cunning rather than introspective or mad. There is a fairly good balance between the physicality of this man of action and the gentler side he subdues as he seeks to avenge his father's murder. At times there is a feeling that Gibson is holding back, worried that he will be accused of doing a *Mad Max*; but it is a pity he does not bring more of that intensity to the role. He does unleash it splendidly, though, in the play's most powerful scene — Hamlet's "refrain tonight" tirade in Gertrude's bedroom. The rage, fear and authority that he, Close and their Italian director achieve here nudge the film towards greatness . . ."

Another tabloid, *The Daily Mirror,* which had always been a supporter of Mel's popular films, was more effusive.

"Mel Gibson's performance is admirable," Bev Tivey noted, "a perfect balance of thinker and man of action. He presents a vigorous, resolute Hamlet, not a vacillating wimp, but a man who knows exactly what he must do, but hates having to do it.''

This review was pinned in Zeffirelli's office, for it exactly hit the mark that the director had aimed for.

With the U.S. and Australia conquered, the promotion swung back to the U.K., where Mel and the director again had special reasons for wanting a hit. After all, this was the home of the language of Shakespeare, where traditionally critics had been least generous to foreign adaptations of his work.

As French journalist, Jacques Le Grossman observed, tampering with such works was on a par with tinkering with the laws of cricket. It just wasn't the done thing. Where Shakespeare had been taught in some American and Australian schools, the British education system made attempts at comprehending the Bard mandatory.

Mel enjoyed the British premiere, attended by the Duchess of York, and waited for the reviews. In London, *The Times* was probably the most important and its' reviewer, carped over Mel's enunciation, saying it had ''the unreal clarity of a speaking clock . . . He (Hamlet) is grave, anguished, tender, playful, all the things Hamlet should be. Yet, though Mel Gibson is never for one moment bad, almost everyone else in the cast is better. And for all his efforts we never get under Hamlet's skin. Mel Gibson's Hamlet appears decent, slick, easily digestible: a fast food Hamlet for the moment, without the stature to make it a Hamlet for the ages.'

The praise was reluctant and strained, but Mel, according to a close friend who spoke to him about the London reviews, was happy that he had gained some respect from critics. Calling his performance ''easily digestible" was fair enough, even if it was alongside the perjoratively used "fast-food". That was exactly what the production was after, a *Hamlet* for the masses.

The Guardian, usually less pompous than *The Times,* commented: "He makes a plain-spoken rather uncomplicated Hamlet who sometimes seems scarcely to know what's hitting him but bravely tries to mould fate to his own ends all the same."

The tabloids were on Mel's side despite the fact that the upmarket reviews were mixed. But it mattered less in the U.K. because it would not take as much effort to attract British audiences.

Testimony to its success in the U.K. was the fact that the country's Film Education Unit asked *Hamlet*'s distributors to get Mel to write a study guide for the movie. They couldn't come to an agreement with him but instead contracted doyen of British literary critics, Frank Kermode, Fellow of King's College, Cambridge to write for the students at 6000 schools which would receive the study.

Kermode, wrote plainly — as Mel himself might have written it. The study acknowledged advantages in the way Zeffirelli rearranged the text. Kermode said Mel was "vigorous and sensitive" Danish Prince.

Later Mel won the Shakespeare Theatre's Will Award in Washington for *Hamlet.*

The theatre's artistic director, Michael Kahn, said Gibson was selected in part because his performance helped introduce film audiences and children to classical theatre.

It's rare that a person with that amount of celebrity will lay themselves on the line," Kahn said, "we were also impressed that Mr Gibson took Hamlet to the classroom in the video called "Mel Gibson goes back to school" (made in Los Angeles with high school students), in which he talks to students about the play and acts out the scenes."

Previous winners of the Will Award, which was established in 1988, included the late director, Joseph Papp, and actors Kevin Kline, Christopher Plummer and Kenneth Branagh. Clearly Mel's decision to play Hamlet was paying off in more ways than he could have anticipated.

During a press conference in the UK, he was asked if his success with the film would mean he would be able to double his fees in the future.

"Not necessarily," he replied. "It takes my average right down . . . You usually operate on how well the last thing did."

Would he be able to return to making films such as *Lethal Weapon?*

"Yeah, why not?" he replied, "There's a lot of money out there to be made. And I enjoy those films."

At the time these questions were being asked his lawyers in Los Angeles were already stitching up an amazing deal which would have given his responses more weight. It was worth about $US75 million and covered a four-picture deal with Warner Bros.

When writer Truman Capote died, his old enemy Gore Vidal quipped acidly that it was "a good career move". The same could be said of Mel taking on Hamlet, except that Mel was very much alive and just thirty-five years of age.

With his Everest conquered, Mel returned to his farm

retreat in Australia to rest and consider scripts his agents were already firing to him for his four movie contract. He was on the biggest roll of his life and he knew it.

CHAPTER
21
LETTING LOOSE

Soon after his exhausting world promotion of *Hamlet,* Mel began attending to many jobs that had been put on hold for months because of his schedule. For instance, he needed to stock up on cattle for his Montana ranch, so he visited Modesto, California to buy a breed he had been after for some time in the U.S.

After a hectic day at sale yards, he went back to his hotel, had a meal and watched TV until he got bored. He was free of minders for the first time in public for months and he just wanted to go out alone and have drink at a bar. He had been encouraged by the cattle sales, where as usual he was recognised but where he had been treated fairly normally, so why couldn't he sneak into a bar for an hour and have a beer or two?

He wandered down to Modesto's East End Bar, sat on a stool and ordered a beer. One turned into four. A barman, realising who he was serving, offered him free drinks. Though why anyone in Mel's situation needed to accept them is beyond comprehension.

"Hey, you're Mel Gibson, aren't you," a tall brunette said, turning many heads at nearby tables.

"I think you're right," Mel said with a grin, and went on drinking. In an hour, the bar was unusually crowded and one member of its staff recalled the place being "abuzz with patrons looking for Mel."

"I couldn't believe how crowded it got," he said. "The manager had to man the door because the bar had filled to capacity."

People were crowding round outside asking if it were really true. Was the Superstar really in there? After about an hour and a half a longer time than he might have been advised to stay there, a photographer arrived just as Mel came out.

"I dunno," a female barworker said, "but he had had quite a few. He had been OK in the bar, didn't say much. People, guys and women were kinda trying to chat to him. He didn't seem to mind. I don't think he wanted to booze all alone. You don't when you hit a bar, do you?"

The photographer positioned himself between Mel and taxi. Mel warned him not to take shots.

"He got angry," a witness, Kelly O'Brien, a Modesto dental technician observed, "not crazy like in *Lethal Weapon*, but angry. I heard him say he would smash the guy's camera if he photographed him. The photographer didn't exactly ignore him, but looked like he took a shot. Mel grabbed the camera and threw it at the guy's feet. It was ruined. Mel staggered to a taxi, got in and left. The photographer was left nursing a shattered lens."

Mel slept off a hang-over, and ventured out for more cattle business around lunch time. He wore dark glasses and hardly said a word to anyone at the hotel.

He ordered a meal to be sent to his room at night and stayed there until about nine p.m.

He became bored again, and decided to have a drink in the hotel's lounge, The Red Lion Inn. He again sat at the bar and was quickly noticed. He started on beer, for which enchanted waitresses wouldn't let him pay. He was soon surrounded by others. Two waitresses, Angela and her roommate, Shawn, in particular paid him a lot of attention.

They were typical of the thousands of busty, young bottle-blondes that serve in bars throughout America, and were forever breathing, 'hey', and 'wow' as they complimented and encouraged Mel, who consumed more and cared less about what was happening. As the minutes ticked by and the drinks went down, the women became more attractive to the celluloid hero, who whether he liked it or not was now getting the adulation he would expect in the US, where actors are Gods — the beings that dreams are made of.

Angela, who was well aware of what was happening to Mel, asked him to join her and Shawn at a favourite after-work haunt of theirs, Miki a Japanese bar and restaurant.

"Yeah, why not," Mel said, looking blearily around at the growing group of admirers. "Let's party."

She then rang her college friend, Wendy Lee Kain. "You'll never guess who's in the Red Lion," Angela said.

"Who?"

"Guess. It's a star. I mean, a big, BIG STAR."

"Madonna."

"No, it's a man. He's coming to Miki's with us. Can you get there? You gotta come."

"I'm coming, but who is it? Who?!"

"Mel Gibson."

"You are kidding!"

"No."

"What's he doing in Modesto? Making a movie? What?"

"You'll never believe it. He's buying cattle for his ranch."

Wendy shrieked.

"We'll be at Miki's as soon as we finish up here. In say, half an hour."

"I'll bring my camera," Wendy said, thinking quickly as she closed the books she had been studying. She hurried to put on make-up.

When Wendy got there Mel had already started on the Saki, and he looked inebriated. She was introduced to Mel, who bowed and kissed her hand. The others got her a drink. The girls had organised it well. They were close friends and now they had one of the great superstars of screen history all to themselves. Miki's was far less crowded, and in keeping with the Japanese, a more sedate place.

Mel felt more comfortable. With his blood-alcohol level rising, he relaxed in the more private and convivial atmosphere without an audience watching his every move. But the booze had already gone to his head and he let go too much. The girls cuddled him and kept up the encouragement, to which he responded. He cuddled and kissed them. He went down on his knees and nuzzled close to Wendy's crotch.

Wendy got out her camera.

"I'd love a picture of you with the girls," she said sweetly, and Mel, in no condition to fight this photographer, shrugged his shoulders and began doing what he does best; he fooled around in front of a camera.

Mel got behind Angela and fondled her. Wendy snapped. Mel posed at the bar with Shawn and Angela, and Wendy took another picture. She then caught a drunken Mel sexily sucking Angela's finger. Next it was two quick shots of Mel and Shawn toasting each other and then downing yet another Saki together.

Mel got right into the swing of it, fell to his knees again and remove Wendy's shoe. He smelt it. He licked it. He panted, growled and barked like a canine, then put the shoe in his mouth, inviting Wendy to snap. She didn't miss the moment and it crossed her mind how valuable the photos might be. "Better be photographed with him," she thought. She handed the camera to a dark-haired male friend, who had also turned up for the occasion. He snapped the three girls with Mel, whose arm was draped around the happily grinning Wendy, her shoe still in his hand.

Wendy got Mel to go down on his knees again. Mel nuzzled into her stomach. The camera snapped again.

The superstar was becoming boisterous as the empty Saki glasses stacked up. The manager said something and the girls thought it wise to whisk their happy hostage away again. He wanted to go back to his hotel, but the girls had other ideas.

Just after midnight they drove Mel to the house Shawn and Angela shared with Angela's fifty year-old father, Fred. The intoxicated four stumbled into the house. Angela took a bottle of Dom Perignon from the fridge and the revelry continued. Mel did a very wobbly Three Stooges impersonation, which caused the girls to roar with laughter. They woke up Angela's dad, who wandered into the living room.

"Dad," Angela said, "meet our good buddie Mel Gibson."

Fred rubbed his eyes and at first didn't believe his daughter.

Gibson bowed and fell back on a sofa, eyes shut.

"You're not as big as . . ," Fred began, before being reassured by all the girls that it really was Mel.

"I've seen the *Lethal Weapon* movies," Fred said, getting over his incredulity. "You were great, just great."

Mel opened one eye and Shawn urged him to do his Three Stooges act for Fred. Mel obliged, overdoing the hair and face rubbing, and causing great mirth amongst the onlookers.

They all drank on. Fred raided his fridge and cellar for the best booze he could find for his famous guest. He soon began to enjoy himself and kept repeating he wished his secretary could meet Mel.

"She's just your most ardent fan," Fred told him.

"Bring her over," Mel urged, slurring his words. Twice he asked where he was. There was just an inkling in the back of his alcohol-soaked brain that this was not the place for him to be.

Fred rang and woke his secretary. He ordered her to come over because he had a very famous, handsome guy at his place, whom he wanted her to meet.

"We gotta do something special," Fred said. "Why don't you get into the closet or something? You know, surprise her."

"You want me to really surprise her?" Mel asked.

"Yeah," Fred urged, backed up by the girls.

"Like in a cake or something?"

They all shouted that this was the right idea.

"You know," Mel began, fumbling for his words, "they usually get women to jump out of a cake, naked. I mean, NUDE, MAN. Like buff-naked."

"Well OK," Fred said. Mel began removing his shirt. The girls screamed in delight. He removed his shoes and socks.

"Hey, let's go," Fred said leading Mel into the hallway, where he stripped to his underpants.

"Where do I hide?" Mel asked. Lights from a car bounced through the front windows.

"Jeez," Fred exclaimed, grabbing Mel by the arm,

"that's her." He opened a hallway cupboard. Mel stepped in.

"Can you fit OK?" Fred asked. Mel could.

Fred greeted his secretary at the front door. She had only just stepped in and was about to ask where the special guy was, when Mel burst from the cupboard without a stitch on.

The woman shrieked and Fred cracked up with laughter as the girls came rushing into the hallway. Fred hurried Mel into a bedroom and threw his underpants and trousers to him. But Mel had had enough. He fell face down on a bed. However, the girls wanted more. They opened the door and had a look. Mel mouthed an expletive, jumped from the bed and staggered out of the bedroom, tripping his way to the living-room. He swiped a bottle of soda from a tray on a coffee table and fell back on a sofa. The others trooped in and gaped as Mel sat drinking the soda. When he had finished the drink he calmly said goodnight and made his way unsteadily back to the bedroom, where he flopped on a bed and quickly fell asleep.

Yet the girls, now all close to being drunk themselves, didn't want to let Mel alone. Angela and Shawn went to the room, opened the door, switched on the light and tiptoed to the bed.

"Mel?" Angela whispered, "would you like coffee?"

Mel however, was snoring soundly. The disappointed girls withdrew to join the others.

Not surprisingly it was a different Mel Gibson who awoke with a splitting head six hours later. He found the bathroom and had a long, hot shower. He couldn't find a towel. Wendy, already awake and dressed, found one for him and had a final look at a naked Mel Gibson.

By a miracle he found his clothes and then Mel dressed and entered the kitchen, where he was greeted by the others.

"Coffee?" Angela asked. Mel grunted in the affirmative and sat at a table. Fred offered to cook up a good breakfast.

"No," Mel said, looking at Fred's watch. "Gotta get back to my hotel."

"We can drive you," Shawn offered.

"No. I'll get a taxi," Mel said as instant coffee was handed to him.

"They take ages," Shawn persisted. "I can drive you."

Mel grumbled a thanks and sipped his coffee.

"Could you give us your autograph?" Angela asked, putting a notepad on the table.

"No way," Mel said, shaking his head.

"Please, Mel," Shawn persisted. "Otherwise no one will believe you were here."

Mel didn't respond. He stared straight ahead, looking gloomy. The others exchanged glances.

"Anyway," Fred said, "it sure was great meeting you."

He reached out a hand. Mel shook it perfunctorily.

"Sure," Mel replied. "Thanks."

Angela asked if he wanted more coffee. He shook his head and stood up.

"Could you drive me now?" he asked.

"Right, Mel," Shawn said. "But how about that autograph, as a momento. We sure enjoyed meeting you last night."

Mel reluctantly took the pad and scribbled his name. As they drove him away, Shawn remarked: ''I don't think anyone will believe you were at our home.''

''Imagine,'' Mel said in a mocking voice as he turned to look at the house,'' Mel Gibson was just in that place.''

Mel later rang his manager and told him of his unfortunate romp. Lawyers were called in. It was decided that one of the girls should be sent a ''Confidentiality and Non-disclosure Agreement'', which demanded that none of them ever disclose any information or pictures for publication. If they did, the legal papers suggested, they would be up for a $50,000 fine.

They realised the value of the illustrated story they had from the night of Mel's drunken indiscretion. Wendy claimed the tale and the snapshots, many of which turned out amatuerishly but publishable, and could be worth a million. She wanted to call Mel's bluff. However, Shawn and Angela felt they had been somewhat responsible for Mel's behaviour, especially having taken him on to Miki's when he was already intoxicated.

Angela consulted her father.

''Leave it be,'' Fred told her. ''So he got a little drunk. I reckon you should let sleeping dogs lie. He had a good time. We had a good time. Basically I really like the guy.''

With that, she and Shawn decided to sign the non-disclosure agreement. But Wendy, the opportunist, who had turned up with her camera, refused to sign it.

''No,'' she told them, ''this is too good a chance to miss. What would a journalist do with the same stuff? He'd publish wouldn't he?''

She engaged a legal representative, who let Mel's lawyers know that he would have to pay to stop her going to a paper with her story. Mel's lawyers called the demands extortion. Wendy's representative claimed his representatives had put pressure on her to sign.

Finally, Mel asked to meet Wendy to talk it over. He flew to Modesto and they met in a coffee shop. He apologised for the way he behaved, and said he was sorry. Mel suggested the night should be forgotten and not brought to public notice. At the end of the meeting, he shook hands with her and wished her the best, believing that it would end there.

However, he had not counted on the determination of Wendy, who wanted payment for her silence. She had nothing to lose. If he didn't pay up, she could go to a paper and get big money for the story, not to mention her fifteen minutes of fame for a drunken, sleazy night with the great Mel Gibson.

The legal wrangling went on expensively for nearly two years before Mel flatly refused to pay up. In stretching it that long, he had minimized the damage any article would have on his career. Fortunately for Mel memories in Hollywood are short and although there were a few sniggers about the episode no serious damage to his reputation or career were sustained.

Wendy's representative hawked the story around and the best offer - rumoured to be six figures — came from American magazines *The Globe* and *National Enquirer*, who defrayed the cost by on-selling the story to several other papers magazines worldwide. Nine photos — including the finger-sucking, the crotch snuggling and the shoe-in-mouth shot — of the night at Miki were published worldwide early in 1993 along with a flimsy text which failed to mention that the event had taken place two years earlier.

Mel felt that the distance of time and the thinness of the tale had been "good damage control", but he had been shaken by what had happened. Friends said he even considered going to Alcoholics Anonymous. The demon booze had caused him enough trouble and threatened his public and private life.

At home, Robyn was incensed over the whole business. Mel swore that he didn't sleep with any of the women. To appease her a spokesman for Mel made a statement to the media saying he did not deny the drinking, but that he was "most definitely denying that any sexual adventures took place".

Mel had learned a tough lesson and soon after the incident he and his management decided that minders would be the order of the day. Since early 1991, Mel doesn't go to a bar or nightclub in the U.S. without someone to watch him and keep any unorganised female company well away. He is left with drunken/womanising dalliances only in fantasies on celluloid.

CHAPTER
22
AS LETHAL AS EVER

"The biggest joke in the movie is that there is any screenwriting credit at all"

A critic on *Lethal Weapon III*

It didn't take Mel much convincing that he should line up for another serve of *Lethal Weapon*. The first two movies had pulled in a reported $600 million, and the producers felt there was a chance to milk the cash cow perhaps just once more.

Mel's fee was said to push through $10 million for the first time in his career and he was to receive a rumoured 10 per cent and a rising percentage of the gross. The temptation was too great, for it meant Mel would have enough power in Hollywood to produce his own films, which would be readily accepted by the major distributors. He had more than paid his dues and was ready. Furthermore, he was well on the way through his relationship with former Sydney accountant, Bruce Davey, with whom he had created Icon Productions, with its office in a small building on the Warner Bros lot. Icon had set-up *Hamlet* and was the catalyst for the four movie deal once *LW3* was completed.

LW3 received scathing reviews such as "*LW3* is like a fusilade of punctuation without any words. Exclamations devoid of context, meaning or impact . . . Perhaps the biggest joke in the movie is that there's any screenwriting credit at all."

And ...

"*LW3* is nothing but another overblown, messy, noisy wreck in which story-telling, character development and dialogue are reduced to insignificance . . ."

And . . .

"*LW3* could have used something, anything, because it has a nonsensical and largely superfluous plot involving confiscated guns being stolen from an LAPD (Los Angeles

Police Department) storage, and something else about real estate . . .''

But it didn't matter. The more the critics ranted, stabbed and attacked the movie, the more the public flocked to see Mel and Danny doing their crazy, monosyllabic thing on the big screen. After *Hamlet,* it was a walkthrough for Mel, who tried hard to make the story more than simply a souped-up parody of itself.

Yet all he had to do was turn up. In the first eight weeks, the third buddy-cop adventure took a staggering $170 million in the U.S. alone, making it the second most successful movie of the year behind *Batman Returns*.

So pleased were Warner Bros, that the studio gave each of the principal cast and crew a new $70,000 Range Rover. Mel, with the prospect of making $30 to $40 million from the third *LW*, was more than prepared for the next stage in his career, as actor, producer and director with control over every film property he could buy.

CHAPTER

23

FOREVER YOUNG AS POSSIBLE

"I can't remember these lines," Mel said to twelve-year-old Elijah Wood during the last day of a fourteen-week shoot. Mel was fatigued and in pain. The kid who had performed excellently throughout the film, was sympathetic:

"Me too. It is confusing. It is."

They were in a cramped tree-house pretending to fly a B-25 bomber.

"I'm not ready," Mel declared, "not in a million years. We'll just be wasting film."

"Well let's just play along with it," Elijah responded, turning suddenly from apprentice into sorcerer. "Mel, if I make a mistake, you just play along, and I'll do the same with you, OK?"

"All right," Mel replied, humble enough to acquiesce where many a big name actor would be too proud, even offended by the kid, no matter how diplomatic he had been.

"You can do it, Mel".

"Thanks."

Forever Young — beautifully shot by Australian cinematographer Russell Boyd — starts in 1939 when test pilot Daniel McCormick (Mel) has a job flying B-25s with the newly formed U.S. Air Corps. His best friend is the brilliant scientist Harry Finley, played by George Wendt, famous worldwide as Norm, the overweight stool-at-the-bar habitue in the TV series, *Cheers,* and his childhood sweetheart Helen (Isabell Glasser in her second feature role, following her debut in *Pure Country*). Daniel's life looks good, especially when he's performing heroics as a test pilot, but he had an emotional — or an unemotional — problem. He can't express his feelings, especially when he needs to when proposing marriage to Helen.

In the film Mel has drawn on his difficulty to confront this fundamental question of life, and has made a romantic film cliché look almost original. He goes weak-kneed in a comical moment when the audience is practically asking Helen for him. Daniel, a born procrastinator concerning matters of the heart, can't do it. He'll try again tomorrow. But there isn't one. Helen is knocked down by a car and goes into a coma. Daniel is devastated. He was never able to express his feelings to the woman he loved.

Grief-stricken, Daniel volunteers for a top-secret cryogenics experiment conducted by his friend Harry. This goes wrong and puts him into frozen slumber for fifty-three years. He awakens in 1992, bewildered, alone and a living anachronism. Daniel's nice guy character, however, is not diminished by time or refrigeration. He stumbles into friendship with a young (fatherless, of course) boy, and the boy's mother, played by Jamie Lee Curtis.

Daniel finds that the opportunity for expressing true love may knock twice, the story's quiet moral being that we should rush to express our emotions, especially in matters of romance.

Director Steve Miner called, "OK, Action!"

The scene started well enough with Mel playing the pilot showing the boy how to fly. But he fluffed his lines. The kid - a true professional — kept going. Mel picked up, but then forgot his lines.

"I'm sorry, really," Mel said, "Basically, I'm confused where I come in."

"Me too, Mel. It's confusing. It's definitely confusing."

Miner called for another take, but Mel became lost again.

"Nurse, doctor," Mel cried, "Help".

The camera crew slumped while Mel went over his lines, checking a few things with Elijah and Miner, who had left it to the actors. There was nothing the director could do. It was a very long, tough scene, yet not beyond professionals.

"Ready to try another?" Miner asked.

"No," Mel said, "I'd like a ten minute break. You'll be just wasting time."

Miner ordered a break. The lights went down. The crew dispersed for a smoke and a soft drink. Mel was left in the dark with Elijah. He read and thought, without saying a word. The kid, understandingly, said nothing for about twelve minutes when he asked solicitously:

"You OK there, Mel?"

Mel didn't respond.

"It's a real tough one, isn't it Mel? Are you OK?"

"I'm OK," Mel replied, sounding a smidgeon despondent. It has been a long shoot, and the actor had let his adrenalin stop pumping about a day too early. On top of that he was suffering from a shoulder which had slipped out of joint during an earlier fight sequence. A chiropractor was expected on the set later during the lunch break. Because of pressures to keep the film on schedule and budget, the production would not stop in the morning, not even for a star in some agony.

Mel grimaced, rolled his head and his eyes, as if summoning an energy rush. The pain was excruciating.

I'm ready,'' he called down to Miner, who signalled for the crew to set up. The lights went on. The set went silent.

Miner chopped his hand.

''Action!''

They performed again, and this time Mel seemed to enjoy it as they slid through unscathed. Seeing the scene in the film, no one, not even the most perceptive pro, would believe that it had not been a breeze for both actors.

Apart from the sheer professionalism of Mel in his nineteenth feature film in fifteen years, that tree-house scene was symptomatic of the film and the better side of Mel's exceptional character and personality. The man is as about as at ease with kids as an adult can be, not simply because he has six of his own with whom he relates so well. He has also retained that childlike sense of enjoyment in life. There was a time in his twenties when he readily admits he lost it. Yet not for long, because by the time he was twenty-five he had a two-year-old with whom he could relate. Then children kept coming through the 1980s, so that when the actor took time out with his family, he was amongst kids again, and as one of eleven himself it was an environment with which he was familiar. His own children wanted him in their world, not be in his unreal, adult existence. He may have given other superficial images to others outside the home, but inside the private boundaries of family life he was a totally loving yet strict dad, a clown and playmate, a great friend and protector. It easily explained why working with kids, even skilled and professionally precocious ones like Elijah, held no terrors for Mel. In the three-hander scenes with Elijah and the impressive young Robert Hy Gorman, Mel, has fun. It's difficult imagining any other big name film actor on the planet, from Jack Nicholson to Arnold Schwarzenegger, or even the exceptionally gifted Robert De Niro, performing better with younger actors. Mel thrived on the challenge.

But revealing, perhaps unconsciously, a streak of insecurity and competitiveness in the context of working with children, Mel said, "I seem to work well with them (kids)." He told a newspaper reporting on *Forever Young* during the shoot, "I think it's because I can make myself more childlike than they. It's pretty hard to steal a scene from me. They've got to get up very early in the morning, I'd say. They talk about not working with kids and dogs. Well, if you are going to work with a dog, act like a dog. If you're going to work with a kid, be more juvenile." In this instance the child actor had, in fact, been more professional than Mel. It must have hurt.

He and Miner — who had a creditable track record with romances and children's stories — both praised their young charges.

"Every once in a while a kid comes along who really understands how to do a scene," Miner expounded. "Someone who can act and doesn't appear to be."

"Elijah seems to have knowledge beyond his years for executing the job," Mel agreed. "He's professional and extremely talented."

Speaking more broadly about his personal relationship with his own offspring, Mel was circumspect.

"Just communicating with kids is tougher than it appears," he told a reporter. "You shouldn't talk down to them, and you shouldn't throw too much at them. You've got to create a balance. You must feel out that balance all the time.''

There was another, possibly even more fundamental reason for Mel's eagerness to take on *Forever Young*, an old-fashioned tear-jerker.

''I wanted to make one I could take the kids to,'' he told the media. ''Some of the others made that difficult. There's nothing better than taking the kids to a good movie that they can relate to, get excited about.''

In this film he had widened his appeal. It would be acceptable to all movie-goers from ages six to ninety. The scene where the boys find the vacuum-cleaner-like cryogenics capsule, would grip any child's imagination.

''It's eerie — a touch of science fiction in a romantic adventure.''

''The kids, as actors, really came to life when Mel woke up after fifty years in the capsule,'' Miner observed. ''It was a wonderful springboard for the relationship he has with these children.''

But the kid's don't have it all their own way. The senior citizens have a few moments too, especially with the concept of finding true love about the time of senility or dotage. It's enough to lift the spirits of every septo or octogenarian.

By making such a widely-appealing show, Mel would lose a few fans by natural attrition in the next few years, but he had increased his kiddie and potential youth vote substantially in one hit, not to mention the support of the great mass of fans in between who wanted a little dose of love fantasy and make-believe to buffer life's truer, harsher, more complex realities.

Mel claims he had much life experience to draw on

here. "I always had trouble building the courage to ask a girl out," he says, "I would work myself up and never quite do it. I'd be so nervous. And then there's marriage. You think dating is difficult? Ha! I had just as much trouble proposing to my wife as I did proposing in the movie. It's hard. It's scary. Not the fear of rejection, but the fear of giving up your freedom. These days though, getting married isn't as "forever" as it used to be. But thirty or forty years ago, "I do" meant forever. These days it's, like, for a couple of years, maybe. It goes against what marriage is supposed to be about."

A technical feature of the film is the fifty-year aging of Daniel and Helen, created by designer Dick Smith and make-up artist Greg Cannom. Daniel ages in six subtle changes.

"With Mel, we tried not to overdo it," Cannom explained. "We wanted him to look very handsome even though he was getting older — a kind of Cary Grant look. But we went very heavy with the aging eye effect because Mel's eyes are so piercing."

Special contact lenses were used to fade the colour of his exceptionally blue eyes three times.

The seven-hour application of heavy make-up allowed Mel to witness his own likely physical maturity.

"It's the best aging make-up I've seen," Mel said after filming. "But I don't think I'm going to look like that. I'll be lucky if I do at eighty-five. Anyway, I won't be acting into old age — unless I age as good as Clint Eastwood. He looks fantastic in *The Unforgiven*. He has aged so well. I bet he could still beat the stuffing out of me in an arm wrestle."

Typically, he fooled around with the aging effect.

"Sometimes I'd wander off the set and go to lunch," he recalled. "People wouldn't know who I was. They reacted very well, and showed the old guy respect."

Mel, then thirty-six, told reporters at a Los Angeles conference that growing old was not a big pressure on him, but said if he had to be frozen, his ideal age, physically, would be thirty-five or thirty-six. Maybe even thirty. Mentally, I'd like to be older, like fifty or whatever. Wisdom, y'know?"

"And after that?" a reporter asked oddly.

"I believe in an afterlife — in a perfect state of being."

"What's perfect?" the reporter prompted further.

"I just know that the things that affect us would not be present in a perfect place."

"Like what?"

"Sorrow. Discontent. Anxiety. Dependence on cigarettes, food or coffee."

Another reporter, appropriately from *Cleo* magazine, wanted to know if Mel would ever have cosmetic surgery.

"I'll never, ever get a facelift," Mel responded emphatically. "I'm never gonna do it. Never. I think people who do that are so pathetic. Pathetic! Why do they do it? What are they worried about? Hey, face it man, Hollwood is more like Holly-weird.

"You go into an old peoples' home and it's frightening. It's like, something from Mars — the living dead! It's awful but the God's truth is — I'm gonna eventually get old, too. So you might as well face it."

Later in an interview with *USA Today*, Mel was more honest, perhaps undiplomatic about his performances.

"I've screwed up in some films and it's not too

damning,'' he said. "I've done some real stinkers. Luckily most were early on."

Mel was asked to be specific.

"I think I did a real bad job on *The River*. When I look at it, I was young and stupid. And I was trying to phone it in, maybe. There were other ones too."

"*Bird On A Wire?*"

"Hmm," Mel agreed.

"*Air America?*"

"Yeah, you got it."

"How did you feel about *Hamlet?*"

"It was OK. We didn't exactly disgrace ourselves."

Like all successful creatives he wasn't reflecting too much on past performances but looking forward to the screening of his next project. It was called *The Man Without A Face*, his twentieth film and the first he had both starred in and directed.

Shot in Maine in the second half of 1992, the story is about a recluse, Mel, who was hideously disfigured by a fire. He befriends a young boy who gradually draws him out of hiding.

He was in the middle of overseeing the film's edit when he paused to promote *Forever Young*. Then it was off to the South of France for a break with his family before starring in a new film with Sissy Spacek, an actress with whom he has a very special rapport, both on and off camera.

During the shooting in July, 1993, Mel heard that sneak preview results of *The Man Without A Face* had topped those of "*Lethal Weapon III*", a tough act to beat in terms of world-wide box-office popularity. His directional debut looked set to do well.

By October, 1993, Mel's concentration was on his next project — *Maverick* the role made famous by James Garner on television in the '50s and '60s.

The character seemed tailor-made for him. Mel has always seemed most comfortable in an all action thriller where he can play a humorous, self-deprecating lad.

At just thirty-seven-years, no one in Hollywood seems to have a better future than Mel Gibson. He's financially secure, even if he never worked again and a most popular person, not just with the paying public, but also with his peers, the media and the people who control the film industry.

The only obstacle, which can stop his continuing achievements, will be his drinking problem. It has caused some much-publicised slips in public places, such as the drunken encounter with the three women in Modesto early in 1991. Yet he seems to have kept the problem under control, without actually beating it. That apart, his 'nice just-one-of-the-guys' image, the on-screen appeal to women for his looks, and the men for his fun/macho style, his undoubted skills, and terrific energy, will ensure a fascinating decade ahead, which could possibly be even more exciting than his first in Hollywood.

INDEX